CHARLES DICKENS

The Last of the Great Men

Charles Dickens, The Last of the Great Men

BY G. K. CHESTERTON

WITH A FOREWORD BY ALEXANDER WOOLLCOTT

THE PRESS OF THE READERS CLUB

NEW YORK

PRINTED IN THE UNITED STATES OF AMERICA

TABLE OF CONTENTS

M 614535

FOREWORD

THIS happiest work by the late Gilbert Keith Chesterton, God rest his soul, is as luminous and infectious a book as ever one author wrote about another. Because the writer of this foreword to the present edition has read that book a dozen times since its first publication in 1906, he feels qualified to describe it as readable—to put it mildly. You will note that Mr. Chesterton himself described it as "a critical study" but, since it involved no study—he knew the material by heart—and is not in the least critical, let us rather call it a hymn of praise, a song of gratitude for such gifts as Charles Dickens and the privilege of being alive.

"The hour of absinthe is over," sang Mr. Chesterton (this was in 1906, of course). "We shall not be much further troubled with the little artists who found Dickens too sane for their sorrows and too clean for their delights. But we have a long way to travel before we get back to what Dickens meant: and the passage is along a rambling English road, a twisting road such as Mr. Pickwick travelled. But this at least is part of what he meant; that comradeship and serious joy are not interludes in our travel; but that rather our travels are interludes in comradeship and joy, which through God shall endure for ever. The inn does not point to the road; the road points to the inn. And all roads point at last to an ultimate inn, where we shall meet Dickens and all his characters; and when we drink again it shall be from the great flagons in the tavern at the end of the world."

On that day in June, 1936, when G. K. C. wheezed his last, I had a notion that there may well have been some little stir in that tavern. I seemed to see a whiskered gentleman, whose gleaming watchfob swung across a waistcoat of unabashed splendor as he hovered expectant around the entrance, making a great commotion about a fire being laid in a room with a bed of extra-size and unusual sustaining power. "I want everything made especially comfortable," he was saying. "This man who's coming is one of us. Besides, he's a friend of mine."

If CHARLES DICKENS, THE LAST OF THE GREAT MEN—he had another book on the subject, compiled of his prefaces to the novels in the Everyman's Library—if *this* Chesterton DICKENS be a critical study, it is the kind that might have been written in an afternoon and evening in just such a Soho restaurant as that one at which he gave me food and drink when I first met him long, long ago. I can imagine him rumpling his hair and splashing good burgundy on the red-checked table cover in the ecstasy of composition, ever and anon calling out, not for a reference work or a document, but just for more copy-paper—and more burgundy. If he needed none of the burdensome paraphernalia or scholarship, it was because this time he was attempting nothing so exigent as a biography and if a word of warning against any passage in this work is obligatory, it is because he did stray into one irresponsible comment on the life of Dickens at a point where he himself was both biassed and ill-informed.

That was in the matter of the Dickens marriage and eventual separation. After his tenth child was born, Charles Dickens was capable of blandly writing to his friend, Forster, that he and Kate had never been meant for each other. But Chesterton was capable of writing that, by a kind of accident, Dickens "got hold of the wrong sister." To offset this oft-quoted nonsense, it is not enough to point out that the other Hogarth girls

were fifteen and eight, respectively, when on the eve of
Pickwick, and in a fever of biological impatience, young
Dickens stepped off to church with their elder sister. It is
necessary to go further and make clear that Charles
Dickens was so neurotically related to the double bed
that any sister he might have married would have been
the wrong one.

But after all, any reader wishing to supplement this
book with a biography of Dickens, must read the letters,
of which the most complete available collection is the
three volumes of them that are part of the recent None-
such Press edition of Dickens. He must also read the
compendious but over-reticent life by the aforesaid Forster. But even when supplemented by a thousand more
incautious footnotes in the 1928 edition, Forster's work
still left something to be said. For example, Ellen Lawless Ternan, the first person after himself whom Dickens
mentioned in his will, was not otherwise mentioned in
the entire Forster life, even when annotated half a century after Dickens had been dust in the churchyard.
The most readily available light on that unimportant
young woman will be found in *Dickens: The Two
Scrooges,* an essay which takes up the first hundred pages
of *The Wound and the Bow* by our own Edmund Wilson. Even that study cannot be recommended without a
warning. In Mr. Wilson's account of Miss Ternan, suspect rumor and sheer conjecture are both offered as if
they were documented fact, so that in that respect, his is
a most *uncritical* study. His Dickens commentary is here
recommended as a corrective to Chesterton. The two
studies differ chiefly in this: it is clear that Mr. Wilson
read his Dickens with scrupulous and unbibulous care,
but in all his hundred pages, there is no evidence that
he ever read Dickens with any enjoyment.

Perhaps this is a book which would be relished the

more by a reader who carried in his mind some picture of the man who wrote it. The late G. K. Chesterton was of such notorious girth that when he tried his hand at the drama, with the odd comedy called *Magic,* Shaw referred to it as Fatty's First Play. But he was also of gigantic height. "Oh, Mr. Chesterton," a young girl once gushed to him, "it must be wonderful to be so famous that everyone knows who you are." "If they don't," he replied sadly, "they ask."

His mild, undisciplined voice was always escaping from his control and breaking into falsetto. I remember how effectively he capitalized this defect when he gave his first lecture in America. Everyone in the auditorium knew who he was, but this didn't prevent the chairman from telling them. That chairman was the late Edwin Markham, famous for having written *The Man With The Hoe.* The distinction of introducing so notable a visitor unhinged Mr. Markham's reason and he embarrassed the speaker of the evening by a bit of florid rodomontade of a sort that had been commoner in the days of Martin Chuzzlewit and Jefferson Brick. It blew up a balloon between Mr. Chesterton and his audience which he had to begin by puncturing. He heaved himself to his feet, strayed to the center of the platform, looked plaintively around him and murmured: "After the whirlwind, the still, small voice."

On that same visit, they led him forth to see the nightly spectacle of Broadway ablaze with a myriad clamorous lamps. "How beautiful!" he said. "How beautiful it would be for someone who could not read!"

I remember fondly my first meeting with Mr. Chesterton in the sultry and unbelievable peace which brooded over London in May, 1914. He gave me lunch in the Soho restaurant aforesaid—a lunch that could last until four o'clock, when he was due at a wedding. For this nuptial flight, I have the impression that Mrs. Chesterton and I got him into a four-wheeler, probably with the use of a derrick and a shoehorn. Before that, for several hours, he held forth in philosophical discourse. I remember that at one point he was discussing the antithetical relation of power and authority. "If a rhinoceros were to enter this restaurant now," he said, "there is no denying he would have great power here. But I should be the first to rise and assure him that he had no authority whatever."

It occurs to me that, from where I sit, I can see that rhinoceros now. At the moment of going to press, he has, thank God, got stuck in the doorway.

ALEXANDER WOOLLCOTT

Charles Dickens: A Chronology

Prepared by Carl Van Doren

1812

Charles Dickens born in Portsea, February 7, 1812, son of John Dickens, a clerk in the British Navy Pay-office, and Elizabeth Barrow Dickens, daughter of a lieutenant in the Navy.

1814–21

Lived with parents in London and Chatham; attended various primary schools; formed ambition to own, some day, the house called Gadshill Place near Rochester, Kent.

1821–24

Again in London, the family in impoverished circumstances; the father for a time confined in Marshalsea prison for debt; the son employed in a blacking warehouse at work he thought degrading.

1824–30

Charles Dickens in boarding school (1824–26); clerk to an attorney in Gray's Inn (1827–28); shorthand reporter for an office in Doctors' Commons (1829–30); in love with a girl who later appeared as Dora in *David Copperfield*.

1831–35

Parliamentary reporter for London newspapers, reporting speeches in the House of Commons and at political meetings elsewhere; wrote and published (1833–35) humorous pieces signed Boz.

1836

Sketches by Boz collected in Dickens's first book; married on April 2, 1836, to Catherine Hogarth, daughter of a London journalist.

1836–37

Posthumous Papers of the Pickwick Club published in monthly numbers, at a shilling each, from March 1836 to December 1837, with immense success; first child born April 1837; *Oliver Twist* begun January 1837 in *Bentley's Miscellany*, edited by Dickens; first visit to France and Belgium in July 1837.

1838–39

Oliver Twist completed and published as book in October 1838; *The Life and Adventures of Nicholas Nickleby* begun in April 1838 and completed in October 1839, in monthly numbers.

1840–41

Master Humphrey's Clock begun April 1840, intended to be a weekly miscellany but largely taken up with *The Old Curiosity Shop* and *Barnaby Rudge,* both published in book form in 1841; visit to Scotland in summer 1841.

1842

First visit to America—Boston, New York, Philadelphia, Baltimore, Washington, Richmond, Pittsburgh, St. Louis, Niagara Falls, Montreal—January to June; *American Notes* published in October.

1843

Martin Chuzzlewit, in monthly numbers beginning January, relatively unsuccessful; *A Christmas Carol,* published just before Christmas, a prodigious triumph.

1844–45

Martin Chuzzlewit completed by June 1844; to Italy in June 1844, to live and travel there till June 1845; *The Chimes,* Christmas 1844; *The Cricket on the Hearth,* Christmas 1844.

1846–48

Residence and travel in Switzerland, June–November 1846; publication of *Dombey and Son,* in numbers, begun October 1846; in Paris, November 1846–March 1847; *The Battle of Life,* Christmas 1846; manager of theatrical company playing in provincial towns, July 1847, April–July 1848; *Dombey and Son* completed March 1848; *The Haunted Man,* Christmas 1848.

1849–50

David Copperfield, in monthly numbers, January 1849–October 1850; *Household Words,* weekly edited by Dickens, begun March 1850.

1851–54

Bleak House, in monthly numbers, begun 1851, completed at Boulogne, August 1853; seventh son, tenth and last child, born March 1853; *Hard Times* written January–June 1854 as a serial for *Household Words.*

1855–57

Lived a good deal in Paris or Boulogne; *Little Dorrit* begun as a serial in *Household Words,* December 1855; bought Gadshill Place, March 1856; *Little Dorrit* completed April 1867.

1858–59

Began public readings from works, April 1858; separated from wife, May 1858; *Household Words* succeeded by

All the Year Round, weekly edited by Dickens, April 1859; *A Tale of Two Cities* begun and completed during year as a serial in the new weekly.

1860–67

Great Expectations, serial in *All the Year Round,* December 1860–June 1861; *Our Mutual Friend,* in monthly numbers, May 1864–November 1865; many public readings from works.

1867–68

Second visit to America, November 1867–April 1868, with profit of about £20,000 from public readings.

1869–70

Edwin Drood, begun October 1869, interrupted after the sixth monthly number by Dickens's death, June 9, 1870; burial in Westminster Abbey, June 14.

The reader who would like to have the complete story of the life of Dickens will find reprinted, at the back of this volume, the succinct and brilliant story of the life which G. K. Chesterton wrote for The Encyclopaedia Britannica.

CHARLES DICKENS

The Last of the Great Men

CHAPTER I

The Dickens Period

Much of our modern difficulty, in religion and other things, arises merely from this, that we confuse the word "indefinable" with the word "vague." If some one speaks of a spiritual fact as "indefinable" we promptly picture something misty, a cloud with indeterminate edges. But this is an error even in commonplace logic. The thing that cannot be defined is the first thing; the primary fact. It is our arms and legs, our pots and pans, that are indefinable. The indefinable is the indisputable. The man next door is indefinable, because he is too actual to be defined. And there are some to whom spiritual things have the same fierce and practical proximity; some to whom God is too actual to be defined.

But there is a third class of primary terms. There are popular expressions which every one uses and no one can explain; which the wise man will accept and reverence, as he reverences desire or darkness or any elemental thing. The prigs of the debating club will demand that he should define his terms. And being a wise man he will flatly refuse. This first inexplicable term is the most important term of all. The word that has no

3

definition is the word that has no substitute. If a man falls back again and again on some such word as "vulgar" or "manly" do not suppose that the word means nothing because he cannot say what it means. If he could say what the word means he would say what it means instead of saying the word. When the Game Chicken (that fine thinker) kept on saying to Mr. Toots, "It's mean. That's what it is—it's mean," he was using language in the wisest possible way. For what else could he say? There is no word for mean except mean. A man must be very mean himself before he comes to defining meanness. Precisely because the word is indefinable, the word is indispensable.

In everyday talk, or in any of our journals, we may find the loose but important phrase, "Why have we no great men to-day? Why have we no great men like Thackeray, or Carlyle, or Dickens?" Do not let us dismiss this expression, because it appears loose or arbitrary. "Great" does mean something, and the test of its actuality is to be found by noting how instinctively and decisively we do apply it to some men and not to others; above all how instinctively and decisively we do apply it to four or five men in the Victorian era, four or five men of whom Dickens was not the least. The term is found to fit a definite thing. Whatever the word "great" means, Dickens was what it means. Even the fastidious and unhappy who cannot read his books without a continuous critical exasperation, would use the word of him without stopping to think. They feel that Dickens is a great writer even if he is not a good writer. He is treated as a classic; that is, as a king who may now be deserted, but who cannot now be dethroned. The atmosphere of this word clings to him; and the curious thing is that we cannot get it to cling to any of the men of our own generation. "Great" is the first adjective which the most supercilious modern critic would apply to Dickens. And "great" is the last adjective that the most supercilious modern critic would apply to himself. We dare not claim to be great men, even when we claim to be superior to them.

Is there, then, any vital meaning in this idea of "greatness" or in our laments over its absence in our own time? Some people say, indeed, that this sense of mass is but a mirage of distance, and that men always think dead men great and live men small. They seem to think that the law of perspective in the mental world is the precise opposite to the law of perspective in the physical world. They think that figures grow larger as they walk away. But this theory cannot be made to correspond with the facts. We do not lack great men in our own day because we decline to look for them in our own day; on the contrary, we are looking for them all day long. We are not, as a matter of fact, mere examples of those who stone the prophets and leave it to their posterity to build their sepulchres. If the world would only produce our perfect prophet, solemn, searching, universal, nothing would give us keener pleasure than to build his sepulchre. In our eagerness we might even bury him alive. Nor is it true that the great men of the Victorian era were not called great in their own time. By many they were called great from the first. Charlotte Brontë held this heroic language about Thackeray. Ruskin held it about Carlyle. A definite school regarded Dickens as a great man from the first days of his fame: Dickens certainly belonged to this school.

In reply to this question, "Why have we no great men to-day?" many modern explanations are offered. Advertisement, cigarette-smoking, the decay of religion, the decay of agriculture, too much humanitarianism, too little humanitarianism, the fact that people are educated insufficiently, the fact that they are educated at all, all these are reasons given. If I give my own explanation, it is not for its intrinsic value; it is because my answer to the question, "Why have we no great men?" is a short way of stating the deepest and most catastrophic difference between the age in which we live and the early nineteenth century; the age under the shadow of the French Revolution, the age in which Dickens was born.

The soundest of the Dickens critics, a man of genius, Mr. George Gissing, opens his criticism by remarking that the world in which Dickens grew up was a hard and cruel world. He notes its gross feeding, its fierce sports, its fighting and foul humour, and all this he summarizes in the words hard and cruel. It is curious how different are the impressions of men. To me this old English world seems infinitely less hard and cruel than the world described in Gissing's own novels. Coarse external customs are merely relative, and easily assimilated. A man soon learnt to harden his hands and harden his head. Faced with the world of Gissing, he can do little but harden his heart. But the fundamental difference between the beginning of the nineteenth century and the end of it is a difference simple but enormous. The first period was full of evil things, but it was full of hope. The second period, the *fin de siècle,* was even full (in some sense) of good things. But it was occupied in asking what was the good of good things. Joy itself became joyless; and the fighting of Cobbett was happier than the feasting of Walter Pater. The men of Cobbett's day were sturdy enough to endure and inflict brutality; but they were also sturdy enough to alter it. This "hard and cruel" age was, after all, the age of reform. The gibbet stood up black above them; but it was black against the dawn.

6

This dawn, against which the gibbet and all the old cruelties stood out so black and clear, was the developing idea of liberalism, the French Revolution. It was a clear and a happy philosophy. And only against such philosophies do evils appear evident at all. The optimist is a better reformer than the pessimist; and the man who believes life to be excellent is the man who alters it most. It seems a paradox, yet the reason of it is very plain. The pessimist can be enraged at evil. But only the optimist can be surprised at it. From the reformer is required a simplicity of surprise. He must have the faculty of a violent and virgin astonishment. It is not enough that he should think injustice distressing; he must think injustice *absurd,* an anomaly in existence, a matter less for tears than for a shattering laughter. On the other hand, the pessimists at the end of the century could hardly curse even the blackest thing; for they could hardly see it against its black and eternal background. Nothing was bad, because everything was bad. Life in prison was infamous—like life anywhere else. The fires of persecution were vile—like the stars. We perpetually find this paradox of a contented discontent. Dr. Johnson takes too sad a view of humanity, but he is also too satisfied a Conservative. Rousseau takes too rosy a view of humanity, but he causes a revolution. Swift is angry, but a Tory. Shelley is happy, and a rebel. Dickens, the optimist, satirizes the Fleet, and the Fleet is gone. Gissing, the pessimist, satirizes Suburbia, and Suburbia remains.

Mr. Gissing's error, then, about the early Dickens period we may put thus: in calling it hard and cruel he omits the wind of hope and humanity that was blowing through it. It may have been full of inhuman institutions, but it was full of humanitarian people. And this humanitarianism was very much the better (in my

7

view) because it was a rough and even rowdy humanitarianism. It was free from all the faults that cling to the name. It was, if you will, a coarse humanitarianism. It was a shouting, fighting, drinking philanthropy—a noble thing. But, in any case, this atmosphere was the atmosphere of the Revolution; and its main idea was the idea of human equality. I am not concerned here to defend the egalitarian idea against the solemn and babyish attacks made upon it by the rich and learned of to-day. I am merely concerned to state one of its practical consequences. One of the actual and certain consequences of the idea that all men are equal is immediately to produce very great men. I would say superior men, only that the hero thinks of himself as great, but not as superior. This has been hidden from us of late by a foolish worship of sinister and exceptional men, men without comradeship, or any infectious virtue. This type of Cæsar does exist. There is a great man who makes every man feel small. But the real great man is the man who makes every man feel great.

The spirit of the early century produced great men, because it believed that men were great. It made strong men by encouraging weak men. Its education, its public habits, its rhetoric, were all addressed towards encouraging the greatness in everybody. And by encouraging the greatness in everybody, it naturally encouraged superlative greatness in some. Superiority came out of the high rapture of equality. It is precisely in this sort of passionate unconsciousness and bewildering community of thought that men do become more than themselves. No man by taking thought can add one cubit to his stature; but a man may add many cubits to his stature by not taking thought. The best men of the Revolution were simply common men at their best. This is why our age can never understand Napoleon. Because he was

8

something great and triumphant, we suppose that he must have been something extraordinary, something inhuman. Some say he was the Devil; some say he was the Superhuman. Was he a very, very bad man? Was he a good man with some greater moral code? We strive in vain to invent the mysteries behind that immortal mask of brass. The modern world with all its subtleness will never guess his strange secret; for his strange secret was that he was very like other people.

And almost without exception all the great men have come out of this atmosphere of equality. Great men may make despotisms; but democracies make great men. The other main factory of heroes besides a revolution is a religion. And a religion, again, is a thing which, by its nature, does not think of men as more or less valuable, but of men as all intensely and painfully valuable, a democracy of eternal danger. For religion all men are equal, as all pennies are equal, because the only value in any of them is that they bear the image of the King. This fact has been quite insufficiently observed in the study of religious heroes. Piety produces intellectual greatness precisely because piety in itself is quite indifferent to intellectual greatness. The strength of Cromwell was that he cared for religion. But the strength of religion was that it did not care for Cromwell; did not care for him, that is, any more than for anybody else. He and his footman were equally welcomed to warm places in the hospitality of hell. It has often been said, very truly, that religion is the thing that makes the ordinary man feel extraordinary; it is an equally important truth that religion is the thing that makes the extraordinary man feel ordinary.

Carlyle killed the heroes; there have been none since his time. He killed the heroic (which he sincerely loved) by forcing upon each man this question: "Am I strong or weak?" To which the answer from any honest man whatever (yes, from Cæsar or Bismarck) would certainly be "weak." He asked for candidates for a definite aristocracy, for men who should hold themselves consciously above their fellows. He advertised for them, so to speak; he promised them glory; he promised them omnipotence. They have not appeared yet. They never will. For the real heroes of whom he wrote had appeared out of an ecstasy of the ordinary. I have already instanced such a case as Cromwell. But there is no need to go through all the great men of Carlyle. Carlyle himself was as great as any of them; and if ever there was a typical child of the French Revolution, it was he. He began with the wildest hopes from the Reform Bill, and although he soured afterwards, he had been made and moulded by those hopes. He was disappointed with Equality; but Equality was not disappointed with him. Equality is justified of all her children.

But we, in the post-Carlylean period, have become fastidious about great men. Every man examines himself, every man examines his neighbours, to see whether they or he quite come up to the exact line of greatness. The answer is, naturally, "No." And many a man calls himself contentedly "a minor poet" who would then have been inspired to be a major prophet. We are hard to please and of little faith. We can hardly believe that there is such a thing as a great man. They could hardly believe there was such a thing as a small one. But we are always praying that our eyes may behold greatness, instead of praying that our hearts may be filled with it. Thus, for instance, the Liberal party (to which I belong) was, in its period of exile, always saying, "O for a Gladstone!" and such things. We were always asking that it might be strengthened from above, instead of ourselves strengthening it from below, with our hope and our anger and our youth. Every man was waiting for a leader. Every man ought to be waiting for a chance to lead. If a god does come upon the earth, he will descend at the sight of the brave. Our protestations and litanies are of no avail; our new moons and our sabbaths are an abomination. The great man will come when all of us are feeling great, not when all of us are feeling small. He will ride in at some splendid moment when we all feel that we could do without him.

We are then able to answer in some manner the question, "Why have we no great men?" We have no great men chiefly because we are always looking for them. We are connoisseurs of greatness, and connoisseurs can never be great; we are fastidious, that is, we are small. When Diogenes went about with a lantern looking for an honest man, I am afraid he had very little time to be honest himself. And when anybody goes about on his hands and knees looking for a great man to worship, he is making sure that one man at any rate shall not be great. Now, the error of Diogenes is evident. The error of Diogenes lay in the fact that he omitted to notice that every man is both an honest man and a dishonest man. Diogenes looked for his honest man inside every crypt and cavern; but he never thought of looking inside the thief. And there is where the Founder of Christianity found the honest man; He found him on a gibbet and promised him Paradise. Just as Christianity looked for the honest man inside the thief, democracy looked for the wise man inside the fool. It encouraged the fool to be wise. We can call this thing sometimes optimism, sometimes equality; the nearest name for it is encouragement. It had its exaggerations—failure to understand original sin, notions that education would make all men good, the childlike yet pedantic philosophies of human perfectibility. But the whole was full

11

of a faith in the infinity of human souls, which is in itself not only Christian but orthodox; and this we have lost amid the limitations of a pessimistic science. Christianity said that any man could be a saint if he chose; democracy, that any man could be a citizen if he chose. The note of the last few decades in art and ethics has been that a man is stamped with an irrevocable psychology, and is cramped for perpetuity in the prison of his skull. It was a world that expected everything of everybody. It was a world that encouraged anybody to be anything. And in England and literature its living expression was Dickens.

We shall consider Dickens in many other capacities, but let us put this one first. He was the voice in England of this humane intoxication and expansion, this encouraging of anybody to be anything. His best books are a carnival of liberty, and there is more of the real spirit of the French Revolution in "Nicholas Nickleby" than in "A Tale of Two Cities." His work has the great glory of the Revolution, the bidding of every man to be himself; it has also the revolutionary deficiency; it seems to think that this mere emancipation is enough. No man *encouraged* his characters so much as Dickens. "I am an affectionate father," he says, "to every child of my fancy." He was not only an affectionate father, he was an ever-indulgent father. The children of his fancy are spoilt children. They shake the house like heavy and shouting schoolboys; they smash the story to pieces like so much furniture. When we moderns write stories our characters are better controlled. But, alas! our characters are rather easier to control. We are in no danger from the gigantic gambols of creatures like Mantalini and Micawber. We are in no danger of giving our readers too much Weller or Wegg. We have not got it to give. When we experience the ungovernable

sense of life which goes along with the old Dickens
sense of liberty, we experience the best of the revolution.
We are filled with the first of all democratic doctrines,
that all men are interesting; Dickens tried to make
some of his people appear dull people, but he could not
keep them dull. He could not make a monotonous man.
The bores in his books are brighter than the wits in
other books.

I have put this position first for a defined reason. It
is useless for us to attempt to imagine Dickens and his
life unless we are able at least to imagine this old atmosphere of a democratic optimism—a confidence in
common men. Dickens depends upon such a compre-
hension in a rather unusual manner, a manner worth
explanation, or at least remark.

The disadvantage under which Dickens has fallen,
both as an artist and a moralist, is very plain. His mis-
fortune is that neither of the two last movements in
literary criticism has done him any good. He has suffered alike from his enemies, and from the enemies of
his enemies. The facts to which I refer are familiar.
When the world first awoke from the mere hypnotism
of Dickens, from the direct tyranny of his temperament,
there was, of course, a reaction. At the head of it came
the Realists, with their documents, like Miss Flite.
They declared that scenes and types in Dickens were
wholly impossible (in which they were perfectly right),
and on this rather paradoxical ground objected to them
as literature. They were not "like life," and there, they
thought, was an end of the matter. The Realists for a
time prevailed. But Realists did not enjoy their victory
(if they enjoyed anything) very long. A more symbolic
school of criticism soon arose. Men saw that it was necessary to give a much deeper and more delicate meaning
to the expression "like life." Streets are not life, cities

and civilizations are not life, faces even and voices are not life itself. Life is within, and no man hath seen it at any time. As for our meals, and our manners, and our daily dress, these are things exactly like sonnets; they are random symbols of the soul. One man tries to express himself in books, another in boots; both probably fail. Our solid houses and square meals are in the strict sense fiction. They are things made up to typify our thoughts. The coat a man wears may be wholly fictitious; the movement of his hands may be quite unlike life.

This much the intelligence of men soon perceived. And by this much Dickens's fame should have greatly profited. For Dickens is "like life" in the truer sense, in the sense that he is akin to the living principle in us and in the universe; he is like life, at least in this detail, that he is alive. His art is like life, because, like life, it cares for nothing outside itself, and goes on its way rejoicing. Both produce monsters with a kind of carelessness, like enormous by-products; life producing the rhinoceros, and art Mr. Bunsby. Art indeed copies life in not copying life, for life copies nothing. Dickens's art is like life because, like life, it is irresponsible, because, like life, it is incredible.

Yet the return of this realization has not greatly profited Dickens, the return of romance has been almost useless to this great romantic. He has gained as little from the fall of the Realists as from their triumph; there has been a revolution, there has been a counter revolution, there has been no restoration. And the reason of this brings us back to that atmosphere of popular optimism of which I spoke. And the shortest way of expressing the more recent neglect of Dickens is to say that for our time and taste he exaggerates the wrong thing.

Exaggeration is the definition of Art. That both

Dickens and the moderns understood Art is, in its inmost nature, fantastic. Time brings queer revenges, and while the Realists were yet living, the art of Dickens was justified by Aubrey Beardsley. But men like Aubrey Beardsley were allowed to be fantastic, because the mood which they overstrained and overstated was a mood which their period understood. Dickens overstrains and overstates a mood our period does not understand. The truth he exaggerates is exactly this old Revolution sense of infinite opportunity and boisterous brotherhood. And we resent his undue sense of it, because we ourselves have not even a due sense of it. We feel troubled with too much where we have too little; we wish he would keep it within bounds. For we are all exact and scientific on the subjects we do not care about. We all immediately detect exaggeration in an exposition of Mormonism or a patriotic speech from Paraguay. We all require sobriety on the subject of the sea serpent. But the moment we begin to believe a thing ourselves, that moment we begin easily to overstate it; and the moment our souls become serious, our words become a little wild. And certain moderns are thus placed towards exaggeration. They permit any writer to emphasize doubts, for instance, for doubts are their religion, but they permit no man to emphasize dogmas. If a man be the mildest Christian, they smell "cant"; but he can be a raving windmill of pessimism, and they call it "temperament." If a moralist paints a wild picture of immorality, they doubt its truth, they say that devils are not so black as they are painted. But if a pessimist paints a wild picture of melancholy, they accept the whole horrible psychology, and they never ask if devils are as blue as they are painted.

It is evident, in short, why even those who admire exaggeration do not admire Dickens. He is exaggerating the wrong thing. They know what it is to feel a sadness so strange and deep that only impossible characters can express it: they do not know what it is to feel a joy so vital and violent that only impossible characters can express that. They know that the soul can be so sad as to dream naturally of the blue faces of the corpses of Baudelaire: they do not know that the soul can be so cheerful as to dream naturally of the blue face of Major Bagstock. They know that there is a point of depression at which one believes in Tintagiles: they do not know that there is a point of exhilaration at which one believes in Mr. Wegg. To them the impossibilities of Dickens seem much more impossible than they really are, because they are already attuned to the opposite impossibilities of Maeterlinck. For every mood there is an appropriate impossibility—a decent and tactful impossibility—fitted to the frame of mind. Every train of thought may end in an ecstasy, and all roads lead to Elfland. But few now walk far enough along the street of Dickens to find the place where the cockney villas grow so comic that they become poetical. People do not know how far mere good spirits will go. For instance, we never think (as the old folklore did) of good spirits reaching to the spiritual world. We see this in the complete absence from modern, popular supernaturalism of the old popular mirth. We hear plenty to-day of the wisdom of the spiritual world; but we do not hear, as our fathers did, of the folly of the spiritual world, of the tricks of the gods, and the jokes of the patron saints. Our popular tales tell us of a man who is so wise that he touches the supernatural, like Dr. Nikola; but they never tell us (like the popular tales of the past) of a man who was so silly that he touched the supernatural, like Bottom the Weaver. We do not understand the dark and transcendental sympathy between fairies and

16

fools. We understand a devout occultism, an evil occult-ism, a tragic occultism, but a farcical occultism is be-yond us. Yet a farcical occultism is the very essence of "A Midsummer Night's Dream." It is also the right and credible essence of "A Christmas Carol." Whether we understand it depends upon whether we can under-stand that exhilaration is not a physical accident, but a mystical fact; that exhilaration can be infinite, like sor-row; that a joke can be so big that it breaks the roof of the stars. By simply going on being absurd, a thing can become godlike; there is but one step from the ridic-ulous to the sublime.

Dickens was great because he was immoderately pos-sessed with all this; if we are to understand him at all we must also be moderately possessed with it. We must understand this old limitless hilarity and human con-fidence, at least enough to be able to endure it when it is pushed a great deal too far. For Dickens did push it too far; he did push the hilarity to the point of incred-ible character-drawing; he did push the human confi-dence to the point of an unconvincing sentimentalism. You can trace, if you will, the revolutionary joy till it reaches the incredible Sapsea epitaph; you can trace the revolutionary hope till it reaches the repentance of Dombey. There is plenty to carp at in this man if you are inclined to carp; you may easily find him vulgar if you cannot see that he is divine; and if you cannot laugh with Dickens, undoubtedly you can laugh at him.

I believe myself that this braver world of his will cer-tainly return; for I believe that it is bound up with realities, like morning and the spring. But for those who beyond remedy regard it as an error, I put this ap-peal before any other observations on Dickens. First let us sympathize, if only for an instant, with the hopes of the Dickens period, with that cheerful trouble of change.

17

If democracy has disappointed you, do not think of it as a burst bubble, but at least as a broken heart, an old love affair. Do not sneer at the time when the creed of humanity was on its honeymoon; treat it with the dreadful reverence that is due to youth. For you, perhaps, a drearier philosophy has covered and eclipsed the earth. The fierce poet of the Middle Ages wrote, "Abandon hope all ye who enter here," over the gates of the lower world. The emancipated poets of to-day have written it over the gates of this world. But if we are to understand the story which follows, we must erase that apocalyptic writing, if only for an hour. We must re-create the faith of our fathers, if only as an artistic atmosphere. If, then, you are a pessimist, in reading this story, forego for a little the pleasures of pessimism. Dream for one mad moment that the grass is green. Unlearn that sinister learning that you think so clear; deny that deadly knowledge that you think you know. Surrender the very flower of your culture; give up the very jewel of your pride; abandon hopelessness, all ye who enter here.

CHAPTER II

The Boyhood of Dickens

CHARLES DICKENS was born at Landport, in Portsea, on February 7, 1812. His father was a clerk in the Navy Pay-office, and was temporarily on duty in the neighbourhood. Very soon after the birth of Charles Dickens, however, the family moved for a short period to Norfolk Street, Bloomsbury, and then for a long period to Chatham, which thus became the real home, and for all serious purposes, the native place of Dickens. The whole story of his life moves like a Canterbury pilgrimage along the great roads of Kent.

John Dickens, his father, was, as stated, a clerk; but such mere terms of trade tell us little of the tone or status of a family. Browning's father (to take an instance at random) would also be described as a clerk and a man of the middle class; but the Browning family and the Dickens family have the colour of two different civilizations. The difference cannot be conveyed merely by saying that Browning stood many strata above Dickens. It must also be conveyed that Browning belonged to that section of the middle class which tends (in the small social sense) to rise; the Dickenses to that section which tends in the same sense to fall. If Brown-

19

ing had not been a poet, he would have been a better clerk than his father, and his son probably a better and richer clerk than he. But if they had not been lifted in the air by the enormous accident of a man of genius, the Dickenses, I fancy, would have appeared in poorer and poorer places, as inventory clerks, as caretakers, as addressers of envelopes, until they melted into the masses of the poor.

Yet at the time of Dickens's birth and childhood this weakness in their worldly destiny was in no way apparent; especially it was not apparent to the little Charles himself. He was born and grew up in a paradise of small prosperity. He fell into the family, so to speak, during one of its comfortable periods, and he never in those early days thought of himself as anything but as a comfortable middle-class child, the son of a comfortable middle-class man. The father whom he found provided for him was one from whom comfort drew forth his most pleasant and reassuring qualities, though not perhaps his most interesting and peculiar. John Dickens seemed, most probably, a hearty and kindly character, a little florid of speech, a little careless of duty in some details, notably in the detail of education. His neglect of his son's mental training in later and more trying times was a piece of unconscious selfishness which remained a little acrimoniously in his son's mind through life. But even in this earlier and easier period what records there are of John Dickens give out the air of a somewhat idle and irresponsible fatherhood. He exhibited towards his son that contradiction in conduct which is always shown by the too thoughtless parent to the too thoughtful child. He contrived at once to neglect his mind, and also to overstimulate it.

There are many recorded tales and traits of the

author's infancy, but one small fact seems to me more than any other to strike the note and give the key to his whole strange character. His father found it more amusing to be an audience than to be an instructor; and instead of giving the child intellectual pleasure, called upon him, almost before he was out of petticoats, to provide it. Some of the earliest glimpses we have of Charles Dickens show him to us perched on some chair or table singing comic songs in an atmosphere of perpetual applause. So, almost as soon as he can toddle, he steps into the glare of the footlights. He never stepped out of it until he died. He was a good man, as men go in this bewildering world of ours, brave, transparent, tender-hearted, scrupulously independent and honourable; he was not a man whose weaknesses should be spoken of without some delicacy and doubt. But there did mingle with his merits all his life this theatrical quality, this atmosphere of being shown off—a sort of hilarious self-consciousness. His literary life was a triumphal procession; he died drunken with glory. And behind all this nine years' wonder that filled the world, behind his gigantic tours and his ten thousand editions, the crowded lectures and the crashing brass, behind all the thing we really see is the flushed face of a little boy singing music-hall songs to a circle of aunts and uncles. And this precocious pleasure explains much, too, in the moral way. Dickens had all his life the faults of the little boy who is kept up too late at night. The boy in such a case exhibits a psychological paradox; he is a little too irritable because he is a little too happy. Dickens was always a little too irritable because he was a little too happy. Like the over-wrought child in society, he was splendidly sociable, and yet suddenly quarrelsome. In all the practical relations of his life he was what the child is in the last hours of an evening party, genuinely delighted, genuinely delightful, genuinely affectionate and happy, and yet in some strange way fundamentally exasperated and dangerously close to tears.

There was another touch about the boy which made his case more peculiar, and perhaps his intelligence more fervid; the touch of ill-health. It could not be called more than a touch, for he suffered from no formidable malady and could always through life endure a great degree of exertion even if it was only the exertion of walking violently all night. Still the streak of sickness was sufficient to take him out of the common unconscious life of the community of boys; and for good or evil that withdrawal is always a matter of deadly importance to the mind. He was thrown back perpetually upon the pleasures of the intelligence, and these began to burn in his head like a pent and painful furnace. In his own unvaryingly vivid way he has described how he crawled up into an unconsidered garret, and there found, in a dusty heap, the undying literature of England. The books he mentions chiefly are "Humphrey Clinker" and "Tom Jones." When he opened those two books in the garret he caught hold of the only past with which he is at all connected, the great comic writers of England of whom he was destined to be the last.

It must be remembered (as I have suggested before) that there was something about the county in which he lived, and the great roads along which he travelled that sympathized with and stimulated his pleasure in this old picaresque literature. The groups that came along the road, that passed through his town and out of it, were of the motley laughable type that tumbled into ditches or beat down the doors of taverns under the escort of Smollett and Fielding. In our time the main roads of Kent have upon them very often a perpetual procession of tramps and tinkers unknown on the quiet hills of Sussex; and it may have been so also in Dickens's boyhood. In his neighbourhood were definite memorials of yet older and yet greater English comedy. From the height of Gad's-hill at which he stared unceasingly there looked down upon him the monstrous ghost of Falstaff, Falstaff who might well have been the spiritual father of all Dickens's adorable knaves, Falstaff the great mountain of English laughter and English sentimentalism, the great, healthy, humane English humbug, not to be matched among the nations.

At this eminence of Gad's-hill Dickens used to stare even as a boy with the steady purpose of some day making it his own. It is characteristic of the consistency which underlies the superficially erratic career of Dickens that he actually did live to make it his own. The truth is that he was a precocious child, precocious not only on the more poetical but on the more prosaic side of life. He was ambitious as well as enthusiastic. No one can ever know what visions they were that crowded into the head of the clever little brat as he ran about the streets of Chatham or stood glowering at Gad's-hill. But I think that quite mundane visions had a very considerable share in the matter. He longed to go to school (a strange wish), to go to college, to make a name, nor did he merely aspire to these things; the great number of them he also expected. He regarded himself as a child of good position just about to enter on a life of good luck. He thought his home and family a very good spring-board or jumping-off place from which to fling himself to the positions which he desired to reach. And almost as he was about to spring the whole structure broke under him, and he and all that belonged to him disappeared into a darkness far below.

Everything had been struck down as with the finality

of a thunder-bolt. His lordly father was a bankrupt, and in the Marshalsea prison. His mother was in a mean home in the north of London, wildly proclaiming herself the principal of a girl's school, a girl's school to which nobody would go. And he himself, the conqueror of the world and the prospective purchaser of Gad's-hill, passed some distracted and bewildering days in pawning the household necessities to Fagins in foul shops, and then found himself somehow or other one of a row of ragged boys in a great dreary factory, pasting the same kinds of labels on to the same kinds of blacking bottles from morning till night.

Although it seemed sudden enough to him, the disintegration had, as a matter of fact, of course, been going on for a long time. He had only heard from his father dark and melodramatic allusions to a "deed" which, from the way it was mentioned, might have been a claim to the crown or a compact with the devil, but which was in truth an unsuccessful documentary attempt on the part of John Dickens to come to a composition with his creditors. And now, in the lurid light of his sunset, the character of John Dickens began to take on those purple colours which have made him under another name absurd and immortal. It required a tragedy to bring out this man's comedy. So long as John Dickens was in easy circumstances, he seemed only an easy man, a little long and luxuriant in his phrases, a little careless in his business routine. He seemed only a wordy man, who lived on bread and beef like his neighbours; but as bread and beef were successively taken away from him, it was discovered that he lived on words. For him to be involved in a calamity only meant to be cast for the first part in a tragedy. For him blank ruin was only a subject for blank verse. Henceforth we feel scarcely inclined to call him John Dickens at all;

we feel inclined to call him by the name through which his son celebrated this preposterous and sublime victory of the human spirit over circumstances. Dickens, in "David Copperfield," called him Wilkins Micawber. In his personal correspondence he called him the Prodigal Father.

Young Charles had been hurriedly flung into the factory by the more or less careless good-nature of James Lamert, a relation of his mother's; it was a blacking factory, supposed to be run as a rival to Warren's by another and "original" Warren, both practically conducted by another of the Lamerts. It was situated near Hungerford Market. Dickens worked there drearily, like one stunned with disappointment. To a child excessively intellectualized, and at this time, I fear, excessively egotistical, the coarseness of the whole thing—the work, the rooms, the boys, the language—was a sort of bestial nightmare. Not only did he scarcely speak of it then, but he scarcely spoke of it afterwards. Years later, in the fulness of his fame, he heard from Forster that a man had spoken of knowing him. On hearing the name, he somewhat curtly acknowledged it, and spoke of having seen the man once. Forster, in his innocence, answered that the man said he had seen Dickens many times in a factory by Hungerford Market. Dickens was suddenly struck with a long and extraordinary silence. Then he invited Forster, as his best friend, to a particular interview, and, with every appearance of difficulty and distress, told him the whole story for the first and the last time. A long while after that he told the world some part of the matter in the account of Murdstone and Grinby's in "David Copperfield." He never spoke of the whole experience except once or twice, and he never spoke of it otherwise than as a man might speak of hell.

It need not be suggested, I think, that this agony in the child was exaggerated by the man. It is true that he was not incapable of the vice of exaggeration, if it be a vice. There was about him much vanity and a certain virulence in his version of many things. Upon the whole, indeed, it would hardly be too much to say that he would have exaggerated any sorrow he talked about. But this was a sorrow with a very strange position in Dickens's life; it was a sorrow he did not talk about. Upon this particular dark spot he kept a sort of deadly silence for twenty years. An accident revealed part of the truth to the dearest of all his friends. He then told the whole truth to the dearest of all his friends. He never told anybody else. I do not think that this arose from any social sense of disgrace; if he had it slightly at the time, he was far too self-satisfied a man to have taken it seriously in after life. I really think that his pain at this time was so real and ugly that the thought of it filled him with that sort of impersonal but unbearable shame with which we are filled, for instance, by the notion of physical torture, of something that humiliates humanity. He felt that such agony was something obscene. Moreover there are two other good reasons for thinking that his sense of hopelessness was very genuine. First of all, this starless outlook is common in the calamities of boyhood. The bitterness of boyish distresses does not lie in the fact that they are large; it lies in the fact that we do not know that they are small. About any early disaster there is a dreadful finality; a lost child can suffer like a lost soul.

It is currently said that hope goes with youth, and lends to youth its wings of a butterfly; but I fancy that hope is the last gift given to man, and the only gift not given to youth. Youth is pre-eminently the period in which a man can be lyric, fanatical, poetic; but youth is the period in which a man can be hopeless. The end of every episode is the end of the world. But the power of hoping through everything, the knowledge that the soul survives its adventures, that great inspiration comes to the middle-aged; God has kept that good wine until now. It is from the backs of the elderly gentlemen that the wings of the butterfly should burst. There is nothing that so much mystifies the young as the consistent frivolity of the old. They have discovered their indestructibility. They are in their second and clearer childhood, and there is a meaning in the merriment of their eyes. They have seen the end of the End of the World.

First, then, the desolate finality of Dickens's childish mood makes me think it was a real one. And there is another thing to be remembered. Dickens was not a saintly child after the style of Little Dorrit or Little Nell. He had not, at this time at any rate, set his heart wholly upon higher things, even upon things such as personal tenderness or loyalty. He had been, and was, unless I am very much mistaken, sincerely, stubbornly, bitterly ambitious. He had, I fancy, a fairly clear idea previous to the downfall of all his family's hopes of what he wanted to do in the world, and of the mark that he meant to make there. In no dishonourable sense, but still in a definite sense he might, in early life, be called worldly; and the children of this world are in their generation infinitely more sensitive than the children of light. A saint after repentance will forgive himself for a sin; a man about town will never forgive himself for a *faux pas*. There are ways of getting absolved for murder; there are no ways of getting absolved for upsetting the soup. This thin-skinned quality in all very mundane people is a thing too little remembered; and it must not be wholly forgotten in connection with a clever, restless lad who dreamed of a destiny. That part of his distress which concerned himself and his social standing was among the other parts of it the least noble; but perhaps it was the most painful. For pride is not only (as the modern world fails to understand) a sin to be condemned; it is also (as it understands even less) a weakness to be very much commiserated. A very vitalizing touch is given in one of his own reminiscences. His most unendurable moment did not come in any bullying in the factory or any famine in the streets. It came when he went to see his sister Fanny take a prize at the Royal Academy of Music. "I could not bear to think of myself—beyond the reach of all such honourable emulation and success. The tears ran down my face. I felt as if my heart were rent. I prayed when I went to bed that night to be lifted out of the humiliation and neglect in which I was. I never had suffered so much before. There was no envy in this." I do not think that there was, though the poor little wretch could hardly have been blamed if there had been. There was only a furious sense of frustration; a spirit like a wild beast in a cage. It was only a small matter in the external and obvious sense; it was only Dickens prevented from being Dickens.

If we put these facts together, that the tragedy seemed final, and that the tragedy was concerned with the supersensitive matters of the ego and the gentleman, I think we can imagine a pretty genuine case of internal depression. And when we add to the case of the internal depression the case of the external oppression, the case of the material circumstances by which he was surrounded, we have reached a sort of midnight. All day he worked on insufficient food at a factory. It is sufficient to say that it afterwards appeared in his works as Murdstone and Grinby's. At night he returned disconsolately to a lodging-house for such lads, kept by an old lady. It is sufficient to say that she appeared afterwards as Mrs. Pipchin. Once a week only he saw anybody for whom he cared a straw; that was when he went to the Marshalsea prison, and that gave his juvenile pride, half manly and half snobbish, bitter annoyance of another kind. Add to this, finally, that physically he was always very weak and never very well. Once he was struck down in the middle of his work with sudden bodily pain. The boy who worked next to him, a coarse and heavy lad named Bob Fagin, who had often attacked Dickens on the not unreasonable ground of his being a "gentleman," suddenly showed that enduring sanity of compassion which Dickens was destined to show so often in the characters of the common and unclean. Fagin made a bed for his sick companion out of the straw in the workroom, and filled empty blacking bottles with hot water all day. When the evening came, and Dickens was somewhat recovered, Bob Fagin insisted on escorting the boy home to his father. The situation was as poignant as a sort of tragic farce. Fagin in his wooden-headed chivalry would have died in order to take Dickens to his family; Dickens in his bitter gentility would have died rather than let Fagin know that his family were in the Marshalsea. So these two young idiots tramped the tedious streets, both stubborn, both suffering for an idea. The advantage certainly was with Fagin, who was suffering for a Christian compassion, while Dickens was suffering for a pagan pride. At last Dickens flung off his friend with desperate farewell and thanks, and dashed up the steps of a strange house on the Surrey side. He knocked and rang as Bob Fagin, his benefactor and his incubus, disappeared round the corner. And when the servant came to open the door, he asked, apparently with gravity, whether Mr. Robert Fagin lived there. It is a strange touch. The immortal Dickens woke in him for an instant in that last wild joke of that weary evening. Next morning, however, he was again well enough to make himself ill again, and the wheels of the great factory went on. They manufactured a number of bottles of Warren's Blacking, and in the course of the process they manufactured also the greatest optimist of the nineteenth century.

This boy who dropped down groaning at his work, who was hungry four or five times a week, whose best feelings and worst feelings were alike flayed alive, was the man on whom two generations of comfortable critics have visited the complaint that his view of life was too rosy to be anything but unreal. Afterwards, and in its proper place, I shall speak of what is called the optimism of Dickens, and of whether it was really too cheerful or too smooth. But this boyhood of his may be recorded now as a mere fact. If he was too happy, this was where he learnt it. If his school of thought was a vulgar optimism, this is where he went to school. If he learnt to whitewash the universe, it was in a blacking factory that he learnt it.

As a fact, there is no shred of evidence to show that those who have had sad experiences tend to have a sad philosophy. There are numberless points upon which Dickens is spiritually at one with the poor, that is, with the great mass of mankind. But there is no point in which he is more perfectly at one with them than in showing that there is no kind of connection between a man being unhappy and a man being pessimistic. Sorrow and pessimism are indeed, in a sense, opposite things, since sorrow is founded on the value of something, and pessimism upon the value of nothing. And in practice we find that those poets or political leaders who come from the people, and whose experiences have really been searching and cruel, are the most sanguine people in the world. These men out of the old agony are always optimists; they are sometimes offensive optimists. A man like Robert Burns, whose father (like Dickens's father) goes bankrupt, whose whole life is a struggle against miserable external powers and internal weaknesses yet more miserable—a man whose life begins grey and ends black—Burns does not merely sing about the goodness of life, he positively rants and cants about it. Rousseau, whom all his friends and acquaintances treated almost as badly as he treated them—Rousseau does not grow merely eloquent, he grows gushing and sentimental, about the inherent goodness of human nature. Charles Dickens, who was most miserable at the receptive age when most people are most happy, is afterwards happy when all men weep. Circumstances break men's bones; it has never been shown that they break men's optimism. These great popular leaders do all kinds of desperate things under the immediate scourge of tragedy. They become drunkards; they become demagogues; they become morpho-maniacs. They never become pessimists. Most unquestionably there are ragged and unhappy men whom we could easily understand being pessimists. But as a matter of fact they are not pessimists. Most unquestionably there are whole dim hordes of humanity whom we should promptly pardon if they cursed God. But they don't. The pessimists are aristocrats like Byron; the men who curse God are aristocrats like Swinburne. But when those who starve and suffer speak for a moment, they do not profess merely an optimism, they profess a cheap optimism; they are too poor to afford a dear one. They cannot indulge in any detailed or merely logical defence of life; that would be to delay the enjoyment of it. These higher optimists, of whom Dickens was one, do not approve of the universe; they do not even admire the universe;

they fall in love with it. They embrace life too closely to criticize or even to see it. Existence to such men has the wild beauty of a woman, and those love her with most intensity who love her with least cause.

CHAPTER III

The Youth of Dickens

THERE are popular phrases so picturesque that even when they are intentionally funny they are unintentionally poetical. I remember, to take one instance out of many, hearing a heated Secularist in Hyde Park apply to some parson or other the exquisite expression, "a sky-pilot." Subsequent inquiry has taught me that the term is intended to be comic and even contemptuous; but in that first freshness of it I went home repeating it to myself like a new poem. Few of the pious legends have conceived so strange and yet celestial a picture as this of the pilot in the sky, leaning on his helm above the empty heavens, and carrying his cargo of souls higher than the loneliest cloud. The phrase is like a lyric of Shelley. Or, to take another instance from another language, the French have an incomparable idiom for a boy playing truant: "Il fait l'école buissonnière"—he goes to the bushy school, or the school among the bushes. How admirably this accidental expression, "the bushy school" (not to be lightly confounded with the Art School at Bushey)—how admirably this "bushy school" expresses half the modern notions of a more natural education! The two words express the whole

33

poetry of Wordsworth, the whole philosophy of Tho-
reau, and are quite as good literature as either.

Now, among a million of such scraps of inspired slang
there is one which describes a certain side of Dickens
better than pages of explanation. The phrase, appropri-
ately enough, occurs at least once in his works, and that
on a fitting occasion. When Job Trotter is sent by Sam
on a wild chase after Mr. Perker, the solicitor, Mr.
Perker's clerk condoles with Job upon the lateness of
the hour, and the fact that all habitable places are shut
up. "My friend," says Mr. Perker's clerk, "you've got
the key of the street." Mr. Perker's clerk, who was a
flippant and scornful young man, may perhaps be par-
doned if he used this expression in a flippant and scornful sense; but let us hope that Dickens did not. Let us
hope that Dickens saw the strange, yet satisfying, imaginative justice of the words; for Dickens himself had, in
the most sacred and serious sense of the term, the key
of the street. When we shut out anything, we are shut
out of that thing. When we shut out the street, we are
shut out of the street. Few of us understand the street.
Even when we step into it, we step into it doubtfully,
as into a house or room of strangers. Few of us see
through the shining riddle of the street, the strange
folk that belong to the street only—the street-walker or
the street arab, the nomads who, generation after generation, have kept their ancient secrets in the full blaze
of the sun. Of the street at night many of us know even
less. The street at night is a great house locked up. But
Dickens had, if ever man had, the key of the street. His
earth was the stones of the street; his stars were the
lamps of the street; his hero was the man in the street.
He could open the inmost door of his house—the door
that leads into that secret passage which is lined with
houses and roofed with stars.

This silent transformation into a citizen of the street took place during those dark days of boyhood, when Dickens was drudging at the factory. Whenever he had done drudging, he had no other resource but drifting, and he drifted over half London. He was a dreamy child, thinking mostly of his own dreary prospects. Yet he saw and remembered much of the streets and squares he passed. Indeed, as a matter of fact, he went the right way to work unconsciously to do so. He did not go in for "observation," a priggish habit; he did not look at Charing Cross to improve his mind or count the lamp-posts in Holborn to practise his arithmetic. But unconsciously he made all these places the scenes of the monstrous drama in his miserable little soul. He walked in darkness under the lamps of Holborn, and was crucified at Charing Cross. So for him ever afterwards these places had the beauty that only belongs to battlefields. For our memory never fixes the facts which we have merely observed. The only way to remember a place for ever is to live in the place for an hour; and the only way to live in the place for an hour is to forget the place for an hour. The undying scenes we can all see if we shut our eyes are not the scenes that we have stared at under the direction of guide-books; the scenes we see are the scenes at which we did not look at all—the scenes in which we walked when we were thinking about something else—about a sin, or a love affair, or some childish sorrow. We can see the background now because we did not see it then. So Dickens did not stamp these places on his mind; he stamped his mind on these places. For him ever afterwards these streets were mortally romantic; they were dipped in the purple dyes of youth and its tragedy, and rich with irrevocable sunsets.

Herein is the whole secret of that eerie realism with which Dickens could always vitalize some dark or dull corner of London. There are details in the Dickens descriptions—a window, or a railing, or the keyhole of a door—which he endows with demoniac life. The things seem more actual than things really are. Indeed, that degree of realism does not exist in reality: it is the unbearable realism of a dream. And this kind of realism can only be gained by walking dreamily in a place; it cannot be gained by walking observantly. Dickens himself has given a perfect instance of how these nightmare minutiæ grew upon him in his trance of abstraction. He mentions among the coffee-shops into which he crept in those wretched days "one in St. Martin's Lane, of which I only recollect that it stood near the church, and that in the door there was an oval glass plate with 'COFFEE ROOM' painted on it, addressed towards the street. If I ever find myself in a very different kind of coffee-room now, but where there is such an inscription on glass, and read it backwards on the wrong side, MOOR EEFFOC (as I often used to do then in a dismal reverie), a shock goes through my blood." That wild word, "Moor Eeffoc," is the motto of all effective realism! it is the masterpiece of the good realistic principle—the principle that the most fantastic thing of all is often the precise fact. And that elvish kind of realism Dickens adopted everywhere. His world was alive with inanimate objects. The date on the door danced over Mr. Grewgious, the knocker grinned at Mr. Scrooge, the Roman on the ceiling pointed down at Mr. Tulkinghorn, the elderly armchair leered at Tom Smart—these are all *moor eeffocish* things. A man sees them because he does not look at them.

And so the little Dickens Dickensized London. He prepared the way for all his personages. Into whatever cranny of our city his characters might crawl, Dickens had been there before them. However wild were the events he narrated as outside him, they could not be wilder than the things that had gone on within. However queer a character of Dickens might be, he could hardly be queerer than Dickens was. The whole secret of his after-writings is sealed up in those silent years of which no written word remains. Those years did him harm perhaps, as his biographer, Forster, has thoughtfully suggested, by sharpening a certain fierce individualism in him which once or twice during his genial life flashed like a half-hidden knife. He was always generous; but things had gone too hardly with him for him to be always easy-going. He was always kind-hearted; he was not always good-humoured. Those years may also, in their strange mixture of morbidity and reality, have increased in him his tendency to exaggeration. But we can scarcely lament this in a literary sense; exaggeration is almost the definition of art—and it is entirely the definition of Dickens's art. Those years may have given him many moral and mental wounds, from which he never recovered. But they gave him the key of the street.

There is a weird contradiction in the soul of the born optimist. He can be happy and unhappy at the same time. With Dickens the practical depression of his life at this time did nothing to prevent him from laying up those hilarious memories of which all his books are made. No doubt he was genuinely unhappy in the poor place where his mother kept school. Nevertheless it was there that he noticed the unfathomable quaintness of the little servant whom he made into the Marchioness. No doubt he was comfortless enough at the boarding-house of Mrs. Roylance; but he perceived with a dreadful joy that Mrs. Roylance's name was Pipchin. There seems to be no incompatibility between taking in tragedy and giving out comedy; they are able to run parallel in the same personality. One incident which he described in his unfinished "autobiography," and which he afterwards transferred almost verbatim to David Copperfield, was peculiarly rich and impressive. It was the inauguration of a petition to the King for a bounty, drawn up by a committee of the prisoners in the Marshalsea, a committee of which Dickens's father was the president, no doubt in virtue of his oratory, and also the scribe, no doubt in virtue of his genuine love of literary flights.

"As many of the principal officers of this body as could be got into a small room without filling it up, supported him in front of the petition; and my old friend, Captain Porter (who had washed himself to do honour to so solemn an occasion), stationed himself close to it, to read it to all who were unacquainted with its contents. The door was then thrown open, and they began to come in in a long file; several waiting on the landing outside, while one entered, affixed his signature, and went out. To everybody in succession Captain Porter said, 'Would you like to hear it read?' If he weakly showed the least disposition to hear it, Captain Porter in a loud, sonorous voice gave him every word of it. I remember a certain luscious roll he gave to such words as 'Majesty—Gracious Majesty—Your Gracious Majesty's unfortunate subjects—Your Majesty's well-known munificence,' as if the words were something real in his mouth and delicious to taste: my poor father meanwhile listening with a little of an author's vanity and contemplating (not severely) the spike on the opposite wall. Whatever was comical or pathetic in this scene, I sincerely believe I perceived in my corner, whether I demonstrated it or not, quite as well as I should perceive it now. I made out my own little character and story for every man who put his name to the sheet of paper."

38

Here we see very plainly that Dickens did not merely look back in after days and see that these humours had been delightful. He was delighted at the same moment that he was desperate. The two opposite things existed in him simultaneously, and each in its full strength. His soul was not a mixed colour like grey and purple, caused by no component colour being quite itself. His soul was like a shot silk of black and crimson, a shot silk of misery and joy.

Seen from the outside, his little pleasures and extravagances seem more pathetic than his grief. Once the solemn little figure went into a public-house in Parliament Street, and addressed the man behind the bar in the following terms—"What is your very best—the VERY *best* ale a glass?" The man replied, "Twopence." "Then," said the infant, "just draw me a glass of that, if you please, with a good head to it." "The landlord," says Dickens, in telling the story, "looked at me in return over the bar from head to foot with a strange smile on his face; instead of drawing the beer looked round the screen and said something to his wife, who came out from behind it with her work in her hand and joined him in surveying me. . . . They asked me a good many questions as to what my name was, how old I was, where I lived, how I was employed, etc., etc. To all of which, that I might commit nobody, I invented appropriate answers. They served me with the ale, though I suspect it was not the strongest on the premises; and the landlord's wife, opening the little half-door, and bending down, gave me a kiss." Here he touches that other side of common life which he was chiefly to champion; he was to show that there is no ale like the ale of a poor man's festival, and no pleasures like the pleasures of the poor. At other places of refreshment he was yet more majestic. "I remember," he says, "tucking my own bread (which I had brought from home in the morning) under my arm, wrapt up in a piece of paper like a book, and going into the best dining-room in Johnson's Alamode Beef House in Clare Court, Drury Lane, and magnificently ordering a small plate of *à-la-mode* beef to eat with it. What the waiter thought of such a strange little apparition coming in all alone I don't know; but I can see him now staring at me as I ate my dinner, and bringing up the other waiter to look. I gave him a halfpenny, and I wish, now, that he hadn't taken it."

For the boy individually the prospect seemed to be growing drearier and drearier. This phrase indeed hardly expresses the fact; for, as he felt it, it was not so much a run of worsening luck as the closing in of a certain and quiet calamity like the coming on of twilight and dark. He felt that he would die and be buried in blacking. Through all this he does not seem to have said much to his parents of his distress. They who were in prison had certainly a much jollier time than he who was free. But of all the strange ways in which the human being proves that he is not a rational being, whatever else he is, no case is so mysterious and unaccountable as the secrecy of childhood. We learn of the cruelty of some school or child-factory from journalists; we learn it from inspectors, we learn it from doctors, we learn it even from shame-stricken schoolmasters and repentant sweaters; but we never learn it from the children; we never learn it from the victims. It would seem as if a living creature had to be taught, like an art of culture, the art of crying out when it is hurt. It would seem as if patience were the natural thing; it would seem as if impatience were an accomplishment like whist. However this may be, it is wholly certain that Dickens might have drudged and died drudging, and buried the unborn Pickwick, but for an external accident.

He was, as has been said, in the habit of visiting his father at the Marshalsea every week. The talks between the two must have been a comedy, at once more cruel and more delicate than Dickens ever described. Meredith might picture the comparison between the child whose troubles were so childish, but who felt them like a damned spirit, and the middle-aged man whose trouble was final ruin, and who felt it no more than a baby. Once, it would appear, the boy broke down altogether —perhaps under the unbearable buoyancy of his oratorical papa—and implored to be freed from the factory —implored it, I fear, with a precocious and almost horrible eloquence. The old optimist was astounded—too much astounded to do anything in particular. Whether the incident had really anything to do with what followed cannot be decided, but ostensibly it had not. Ostensibly the cause of Charles's ultimate liberation was a quarrel between his father and Lamert, the head of the factory. Dickens the elder (who had at last left the Marshalsea) could no doubt conduct a quarrel with the magnificence of Micawber; the result of this talent, at any rate, was to leave Mr. Lamert in a towering rage. He had a stormy interview with Charles, in which he tried to be good-tempered to the boy, but could hardly master his tongue about the boy's father. Finally he told him he must go, and with every observance the little creature was solemnly expelled from hell.

His mother, with a touch of strange harshness, was for patching up the quarrel and sending him back. Perhaps, with the fierce feminine responsibility, she felt that the first necessity was to keep the family out of debt. But old John Dickens put his foot down here— put his foot down with that ringing but very rare decision with which (once in ten years, and often on some trivial matter) the weakest man will overwhelm the strongest woman. The boy was miserable; the boy was clever; the boy should go to school. The boy went to school; he went to the Wellington House Academy, Mornington Place. It was an odd experience for any one to go from the world to a school, instead of going from school to the world. Dickens, we may say, had his boyhood after his youth. He had seen life at its coarsest before he began his training for it, and knew the worst words in the English language probably before the best. This odd chronology, it will be remembered, he retained in his semi-autobiographical account of the adventures of David Copperfield, who went into the business of Murdstone and Grinby's before he went to the school kept by Dr. Strong. David Copperfield, also, went to be carefully prepared for a world that he had seen already. Outside David Copperfield, the records of Dickens at this time reduce themselves to a few glimpses provided by accidental companions of his schooldays, and little can be deduced from them about his personality beyond a general impression of sharpness and, perhaps, of bravado, of bright eyes and bright speeches. Probably the young creature was recuperating himself for his misfortunes, was making the most of his liberty, was flapping the wings of that wild spirit that had just not been broken. We hear of things that sound suddenly juvenile after his maturer troubles, of a secret language sounding like mere gibberish, and of a small theatre, with paint and red fire, such as that which Stevenson loved. It was not an accident that Dickens and Stevenson loved it. It is a stage unsuited for psychological realism; the cardboard characters cannot analyze each other with any effect. But it is a stage almost divinely suited for making surroundings, for making that situation and background which belong peculiarly to romance. A toy theatre, in fact, is the opposite of private theatricals. In the latter you can do anything with the people if you do not ask much from the scenery; in the former you can do anything in scenery if you do not ask much from the people. In a toy theatre you could hardly manage a modern dialogue on marriage, but the Day of Judgment would be quite easy.

After leaving school, Dickens found employment as a clerk to Mr. Blackmore, a solicitor, as one of those inconspicuous under-clerks whom he afterwards turned to many grotesque uses. Here, no doubt, he met Lowten and Swiveller, Chuckster and Wobbler, in so far as such sacred creatures ever had embodiments on this lower earth. But it is typical of him that he had no fancy at all to remain a solicitor's clerk. The resolution to rise which had glowed in him even as a dawdling boy, when he gazed at Gad's-hill, which had been darkened but not quite destroyed by his fall into the factory routine, which had been released again by his return to normal boyhood and the boundaries of school, was not likely to content itself now with the copying out of agreements. He set to work, without any advice or help, to learn to be a reporter. He worked all day at law, and then all night at shorthand. It is an art which can only be effected by time, and he had to effect it by overtime. But learning the thing under every disadvantage, without a teacher, without the possibility of concentration or complete mental force, without ordinary human sleep, he made himself one of the most rapid reporters then alive. There is a curious contrast between the casualness of the mental training to which his parents and others subjected him and the savage seriousness of the training to which he subjected himself. Somebody once asked old John Dickens where his son Charles was educated. "Well, really," said the great creature, in his spacious way, "he may be said—ah—to have educated himself." He might indeed.

This practical intensity of Dickens is worth our dwelling on, because it illustrates an elementary antithesis in his character, or what appears as an antithesis in our modern popular psychology. We are always talking about strong men against weak men; but Dickens was not only both a weak man and a strong man, he was a very weak man and also a very strong man. He was everything that we currently call a weak man; he was a man hung on wires; he was a man who might at any moment cry like a child; he was so sensitive to criticism that one may say that he lacked a skin; he was so nervous that he allowed great tragedies in his life to arise only out of nerves. But in the matter where all ordinary strong men are miserably weak—in the matter of concentrated toil and clear purpose and unconquerable worldly courage—he was like a straight sword. Mrs. Carlyle, who in her human epithets often hit the right nail so that it rang, said of him once, "He has a face made of steel." This was probably felt in a flash when she saw, in some social crowd, the clear, eager face of Dickens cutting through those near him like a knife. Any people who had met him from year to year would each year have found a man weakly troubled about his worldly decline; and each year they would have found him higher up in the world. His was a character very hard for any man of slow and placable temperament to understand; he was the character whom anybody can hurt and nobody can kill.

When he began to report in the House of Commons he was still only nineteen. His father, who had been released from his prison a short time before Charles had been released from his, had also become, among many other things, a reporter. But old John Dickens could enjoy doing anything without any particular aspiration after doing it well. But Charles was of a very different temper. He was, as I have said, consumed with an enduring and almost angry thirst to excel. He learnt shorthand with a dark self-devotion as if it were a sacred hieroglyph. Of this self-instruction, as of everything else, he has left humorous and illuminating phrases. He describes how, after he had learnt the whole exact alphabet, "there then appeared a procession of new horrors, called arbitrary characters—the most despotic characters I have ever known; who insisted, for instance, that a thing like the beginning of a cobweb meant 'expectation,' and that a pen-and-ink skyrocket stood for 'disadvantageous.' " He concludes, "It was almost heartbreaking." But it is significant that somebody else, a colleague of his, concluded, "There never *was* such a shorthand writer."

Dickens succeeded in becoming a shorthand writer; succeeded in becoming a reporter; succeeded ultimately in becoming a highly effective journalist. He was appointed as a reporter of the speeches in Parliament, first by *The True Sun,* then by *The Mirror of Parliament,* and last by *The Morning Chronicle.* He reported the speeches very well, and if we must analyze his internal opinions, much better than they deserved. For it must be remembered that this lad went into the reporter's gallery full of the triumphant Radicalism which was then the rising tide of the world. He was, it must be confessed, very little overpowered by the dignity of the Mother of Parliaments: he regarded the House of Commons much as he regarded the House of Lords, as a sort of venerable joke. It was, perhaps, while he watched, pale with weariness from the reporter's gallery, that there sank into him a thing that never left him, his unfathomable contempt for the British constitution. Then perhaps he heard from the Government benches the immortal apologies of the Circumlocution Office. "Then would the noble lord or right honourable gentleman, in whose department it was to defend the Circumlocution Office, put an orange in his pocket, and make a regular field-day of the occasion. Then would he come down to that house with a slap upon the table and meet the honourable gentleman foot to foot. Then would he be there to tell that honourable gentleman that the Circumlocution Office was not only blameless in this matter, but was commendable in this matter, was extollable to the skies in this matter. Then would he be there to tell that honourable gentleman that although the Circumlocution Office was invariably right, and wholly right, it never was so right as in this matter. Then would he be there to tell the honourable gentleman that it would have been more to his honour, more to his credit, more to his good taste, more to his good sense, more to half the dictionary of commonplaces if he had left the Circumlocution Office alone and never approached this matter. Then would he keep one eye upon a coach or crammer from the Circumlocution Office below the bar, and smash the honourable gentleman with the Circumlocution Office account of this matter. And although one of two things always happened; namely, either that the Circumlocution Office had nothing to say, and said it, or that it had something to say of which the noble lord or right honourable gentleman blundered one half and forgot the other; the Circumlocution Office was always voted immaculate by an accommodating majority." We are now generally told that Dickens has destroyed these abuses, and that this is no longer a true picture of public life. Such, at any rate, is the Circumlocution Office account of this matter. But Dickens as a good Radical would, I fancy, much prefer that we should continue his battle than that we should celebrate his triumph; especially when it has not come. England is still ruled by the great Barnacle family. Parliament is still ruled by the great Barnacle trinity—the solemn old Barnacle, who knew that the Circumlocution Office was a protection, the sprightly young Barnacle who knew that it was a fraud, and the bewildered young Barnacle who knew nothing about it. From these three types our Cabinets are still exclusively recruited. People talk of the tyrannies and anomalies which Dickens denounced as things of the past like the Star Chamber. They believe that the days of the old stupid optimism and the old brutal indifference are gone for ever. In truth, this very belief is only the continuance of the old stupid optimism and the old brutal indifference. We believe in a free England and a pure England, because we still believe in the Circumlocution Office account of this matter. Undoubtedly our serenity is wide-spread. We believe that England is really reformed, we believe that England is really democratic, we believe that English politics are free from corruption. But this general satisfaction of ours does not show that Dickens has beaten the Barnacles. It only shows that the Barnacles have beaten Dickens.

It cannot be too often said, then, that we must read into young Dickens and his works this old Radical tone towards institutions. That tone was a sort of happy impatience. And when Dickens had to listen for hours to the speech of the noble lord in defence of the Circumlocution Office, when, that is, he had to listen to what he regarded as the last vapourings of a vanishing oligarchy, the impatience rather predominated over the happiness. His incurably restless nature found more pleasure in the wandering side of journalism. He went about wildly in post-chaises to report political meetings

47

for the *Morning Chronicle*. "And what gentlemen they were to serve," he exclaimed, "in such things at the old *Morning Chronicle*. Great or small it did not matter. I have had to charge for half a dozen breakdowns in half a dozen times as many miles. I have had to charge for the damage of a great-coat from the drippings of a blazing wax candle, in writing through the smallest hours of the night in a swift flying carriage and pair." And again, "I have often transcribed for the printer from my short-hand notes important public speeches in which the strictest accuracy was required, and a mistake in which would have been to a young man severely compromising, writing on the palm of my hand, by the light of a dark lantern, in a post-chaise and four, galloping through a wild country and through the dead of the night, at the then surprising rate of fifteen miles an hour." The whole of Dickens's life goes with the throb of that nocturnal gallop. All its real wildness shot through with an imaginative wickedness he afterwards uttered in the drive of Jonas Chuzzlewit through the storm.

All this time, and indeed from a time of which no measure can be taken, the creative part of his mind had been in a stir or even a fever. While still a small boy he had written for his own amusement some sketches of queer people he had met; notably, one of his uncle's barber, whose principal hobby was pointing out what Napoleon ought to have done in the matter of military tactics. He had a note-book full of such sketches. He had sketches not only of persons, but of places which were to him almost more personal than persons. In the December of 1833 he published one of these fragments in the *Old Monthly Magazine*. This was followed by nine others in the same paper, and when the paper (which was a romantically Radical venture, run by a veteran soldier of Bolivar) itself collapsed, Dickens continued the series in the *Evening Chronicle,* an off-shoot of the morning paper of the same name. These were the pieces afterwards published and known as the "Sketches by Boz"; and with them Dickens enters literature. He also enters many other things about this time; he enters manhood, and among other things marriage. A friend of his on the *Chronicle,* George Hogarth, had several daughters. With all of them Dickens appears to have been on terms of great affection. This sketch is wholly literary, and I do not feel it necessary to do more than touch upon such incidents as his marriage, just as I shall do no more than touch upon the tragedy that ultimately overtook it. But it may be suggested here that the final misfortunes were in some degree due to the circumstances attending the original action. A very young man fighting his way, and excessively poor, with no memories for years past that were not monotonous and mean, and with his strongest and most personal memories quite ignominious and unendurable, was suddenly thrown into the society of a whole family of girls. I think it does not overstate his weakness, and I think it partly constitutes his excuse, to say that he fell in love with all of them. As sometimes happens in the undeveloped youth, an abstract femininity simply intoxicated him. And again, I think we shall not be mistakenly accused of harshness if we put the point in this way; that by a kind of accident he got hold of the wrong sister. In what came afterwards he was enormously to blame. But I do not think that his was a case of cold division from a woman whom he had once seriously and singly loved. He had been bewildered in a burning haze, I will not say even of first love, but of first flirtations. His wife's sisters stimulated him before he fell in love with his wife; and they continued to stimulate him long after he had quarrelled with her for ever. This view is strikingly supported by all the details of his attitude towards all the other members of the sacred house of Hogarth. One of the sisters remained, of course, his dearest friend till death. Another who had died, he worshipped as a saint, and he always asked to be buried in her grave. He was married on April 2, 1836. Forster remarks that a few days before the announcement of their marriage in the *Times,* the same paper contained another announcement that on the 31st would be published the first number of a work called "The Posthumous Papers of the Pickwick Club." It is the beginning of his career.

The "Sketches," apart from splendid splashes of humour here and there, are not manifestations of the man of genius. We might almost say that this book is one of the few books by Dickens which would not, standing alone, have made his fame. And yet standing alone it did make his fame. His contemporaries could see a new spirit in it, where we, familiar with the larger fruits of that spirit, can only see a continuation of the prosaic and almost wooden wit of the comic books of that day. But in any case we should hardly look in the man's first book for the fulness of his contribution to letters. Youth is almost everything else, but it is hardly ever original. We read of young men bursting on the old world with a new message. But youth in actual experience is the period of imitation and even obedience. Subjectively its emotions may be furious and headlong; but its only external outcome is a furious imitation and a headlong obedience. As we grow older we learn the special thing we have to do. As a man goes on towards the grave he discovers gradually a philosophy he can really call fresh, a style he can really call his own, and as he becomes an older man he becomes a newer writer. Ibsen, in his youth, wrote almost classic plays about vikings; it was in his old age that he began to break windows and throw fireworks. The only fault, it was said, of Browning's first poems was that they had "too much beauty of imagery, and too little wealth of thought." The only fault, that is, of Browning's first poems, was that they were not Browning's.

In one way, however, the "Sketches by Boz" do stand out very symbolically in the life of Dickens. They constitute in a manner the dedication of him to his especial task; the sympathetic and yet exaggerated painting of the poorer middle class. He was to make men feel that this dull middle class was actually a kind of Elfland. But here, again, the work is rude and undeveloped; and this is shown in the fact that it is a great deal more exaggerative than it is sympathetic. We are not, of course, concerned with the kind of people who say that they wish that Dickens was more refined. If those people are ever refined it will be by fire. But there is in this earliest work, an element which almost vanished in the later ones, an element which is typical of the middle classes in England, and which is in a more real sense to be called vulgar. I mean that in these little farces there is a trace, in the author as well as in the characters, of that petty sense of social precedence, that hub-hub of little unheard-of oligarchies, which is the only serious sin of the bourgeoisie of Britain. It may seem pragmatical, for example, to instance such a rowdy farce as the story of Horatio Sparkins, which tells how a tuft-hunting family entertained a rhetorical youth thinking he was a lord, and found he was a draper's assistant. No doubt they were very snobbish in thinking that a lord must be eloquent; but we cannot help feeling that Dickens is almost equally snobbish in feeling it so very funny that a draper's assistant should be eloquent. A free man, one would think, would despise the family quite as much if

Horatio had been a peer. Here, and here only, there is just a touch of the vulgarity, of the only vulgarity of the world out of which Dickens came. For the only element of lowness that there really is in our populace is exactly that they are full of superiorities and very conscious of class. Shades, imperceptible to the eyes of others, but as hard and haughty as a Brahmin caste, separate one kind of charwoman from another kind of charwoman. Dickens was destined to show with inspired symbolism all the immense virtues of the democracy. He was to show them as the most humorous part of our civilization; which they certainly are. He was to show them as the most promptly and practically compassionate part of our civilization; which they certainly are. The democracy has a hundred exuberant good qualities; the democracy has only one outstanding sin—it is not democratic.

CHAPTER IV

"*The Pickwick Papers*"

Round the birth of "Pickwick" broke one of those literary quarrels that were too common in the life of Dickens. Such quarrels indeed generally arose from some definite mistake or misdemeanour on the part of somebody else; but they were also made possible by an indefinite touchiness and susceptibility in Dickens himself. He was so sensitive on points of personal authorship and responsibility that even his sacred sense of humour deserted him. He turned people into mortal enemies whom he might have turned very easily into immortal jokes. It was not that he was lawless: in a sense it was that he was too legal; but he did not understand the principle of *de minimis non curat lex*. Anybody could draw him; any fool could make a fool of him. Any obscure madman who chose to say that he had written the whole of "Martin Chuzzlewit"; any penny-a-liner who chose to say that Dickens wore no shirt collar could call forth the most passionate and public denials as of a man pleading "not guilty" to witchcraft or high treason. Hence the letters of Dickens are filled with a certain singular type of quarrels and complaints, quarrels and complaints in which one cannot say that he was on the wrong side, but merely that even in being on the right side he was in the wrong place. He was not only a generous man, he was even a just man; to have made against anybody a charge or claim which was unfair would have been insupportable to him. His weakness was that he found the unfair claim or charge, however small, equally insupportable when brought against himself. No one can say of him that he was often wrong; we can only say of him as of many pugnacious people, that he was too often right.

The incidents attending the inauguration of "The Pickwick Papers" are not, perhaps, a perfect example of this trait, because Dickens was here a hand-to-mouth journalist, and the blow might possibly have been more disabling than those struck at him in his days of triumph. But all through those days of triumph, and to the day of his death, Dickens took this old tea-cup tempest with the most terrible gravity, drew up declarations, called witnesses, preserved pulverizing documents, and handed on to his children the forgotten folly as if it had been a Highland feud. Yet the unjust claim made on him was so much more ridiculous even than it was unjust, that it seems strange that he should have remembered it for a month except for his amusement. The facts are simple and familiar to most people. The publishers—Chapman & Hall—wished to produce some kind of serial with comic illustrations by a popular caricaturist named Seymour. This artist was chiefly famous for his rendering of the farcical side of sport, and to suit this specialty it was very vaguely suggested to Dickens by the publishers that he should write about a Nimrod Club, or some such thing, a club of amateur sportsmen, foredoomed to perpetual ignominies. Dickens objected in substance upon two very sensible grounds—first, that sporting sketches were stale; and second, that he knew nothing about sport. He changed the idea to that of a general club for travel and investigation, the Pickwick Club, and only retained one fated sportsman, Mr. Winkle, the melancholy remnant of the Nimrod Club that never was. The first seven pictures appeared with the signature of Seymour and the letterpress of Dickens, and in them Winkle and his woes were fairly, but not extraordinarily prominent. Before the eighth picture appeared Seymour had blown his brains out. After a brief interval of the employment of a man named Buss, Dickens obtained the assistance of Hablot K. Browne whom we all call "Phiz," and may almost, in a certain sense, be said to have gone into partnership with him. They were as suited to each other and to the common creation of a unique thing as Gilbert and Sullivan. No other illustrator ever created the true Dickens characters with the precise and correct quantum of exaggeration. No other illustrator ever breathed the true Dickens atmosphere, in which clerks are clerks and yet at the same time elves.

To the tame mind the above affair does not seem to offer anything very promising in the way of a row. But Seymour's widow managed to evolve out of it the proposition that somehow or other her husband had written "Pickwick," or, at least, had been responsible for the genius and success of it. It does not appear that she had anything at all resembling a reason for this opinion except the unquestionable fact that the publishers had started with the idea of employing Seymour. This was quite true, and Dickens (who over and above his honesty was far too quarrelsome a man not to try to keep in the right, and who showed a sort of fierce carefulness in telling the truth in such cases) never denied it or attempted to conceal it. It was quite true, that at the beginning, instead of Seymour being employed to illustrate Dickens, Dickens may be said to have been employed to illustrate Seymour. But that Seymour invented anything in the letterpress large or small, that he invented either the outline of Mr. Pickwick's character or the number of Mr. Pickwick's cabman, that he invented either the story, or so much as a semi-colon in the story was not only never proved, but was never very lucidly alleged. Dickens fills his letters with all that there is to be said against Mrs. Seymour's idea; it is not very clear whether there was ever anything definitely said for it.

Upon the mere superficial fact and law of the affair, Dickens ought to have been superior to this silly business. But in a much deeper and a much more real sense he ought to have been superior to it. It did not really touch him or his greatness at all, even as an abstract allegation. If Seymour had started the story, had provided Dickens with his puppets, Tupman or Jingle, Dickens would have still have been Dickens and Seymour only Seymour. As a matter of fact, it happened to be a contemptible lie, but it would have been an equally contemptible truth. For the fact is that the greatness of Dickens and especially the greatness of Pickwick is not of a kind that could be affected by somebody else suggesting the first idea. It could not be affected by somebody else writing the first chapter. If it could be shown that another man had suggested to Hawthorne (let us say) the primary conception of the "Scarlet Letter," Hawthorne who worked it out would still be an exquisite workman; but he would be by so much less a creator. But in a case like Pickwick there is a simple test. If Seymour gave Dickens the main idea of Pickwick, what was it? There is no primary conception of Pickwick for any one to suggest. Dickens not only did not get the general plan from Seymour, he did not get it at all. In Pickwick, and, indeed, in Dickens, generally it is in the details that the author is creative, it is in the details that he is vast. The power of the book lies in the perpetual torrent of ingenious and inventive treatment; the theme (at least at the beginning) simply does not exist. The idea of Tupman, the fat lady-killer, is in itself quite dreary and vulgar; it is the detailed Tupman, as he is developed, who is unexpectedly amusing. The idea of Winkle, the clumsy sportsman, is in itself quite stale; it is as he goes on repeating himself that he becomes original. We hear of men whose imagination can touch with magic the dull facts of our life, but Dickens's yet more indomitable fancy could touch with magic even our dull fiction. Before we are halfway through the book the stock characters of dead and damned farces astonish us like splendid strangers.

Seymour's claim, then, viewed symbolically was even a compliment. It was true in spirit that Dickens obtained (or might have obtained) the start of Pickwick from somebody else, from anybody else. For he had a more gigantic energy than the energy of the intense artist, the energy which is prepared to write something. He had the energy which is prepared to write anything. He could have finished any man's tale. He could have breathed a mad life into any man's characters. If it had been true that Seymour had planned out Pickwick, if Seymour had fixed the chapters and named and numbered the characters, his slave would have shown even in these shackles such a freedom as would have shaken the world. If Dickens had been forced to make his incidents out of a chapter in a child's reading-book, or the names in a scrap of newspaper, he would have turned them in ten pages into creatures of his own. Seymour, as I say, was in a manner right in spirit. Dickens would at this time get his materials from anywhere, in the sense

57

that he cared little what materials they were. He would not have stolen; but if he had stolen he would never have imitated. The power which he proceeded at once to exhibit was the one power in letters which literally cannot be imitated, the primary inexhaustible creative energy, the enormous prodigality of genius which no one but another genius could parody. To claim to have originated an idea of Dickens is like claiming to have contributed a glass of water to Niagara. Wherever this stream or that stream started the colossal cataract of absurdity went roaring night and day. The volume of his invention overwhelmed all doubt of his inventiveness; Dickens was evidently a great man; unless he was a thousand men.

The actual circumstances of the writing and publishing of "Pickwick" show that while Seymour's specific claim was absurd, Dickens's indignant exactitude about every jot and tittle of authorship was also inappropriate and misleading. "The Pickwick Papers," when all is said and done, did emerge out of a haze of suggestions and proposals in which more than one person was involved. The publishers failed to base the story on a Nimrod Club, but they succeeded in basing it on a club. Seymour, by virtue of his idiosyncrasy, if he did not create, brought about the creation of Mr. Winkle. Seymour sketched Mr. Pickwick as a tall, thin man. Mr. Chapman (apparently without any word from Dickens) boldly turned him into a short, fat man. Chapman took the type from a corpulent old dandy named Foster, who wore tights and gaiters and lived at Richmond. In this sense, were we affected by this idle aspect of the thing, we might call Chapman the real originator of "Pickwick." But as I have suggested, originating "Pickwick" is not the point. It was quite easy to originate "Pickwick." The difficulty was to write it.

However such things may be, there can be no question of the result of this chaos. In "The Pickwick Papers" Dickens sprang suddenly from a comparatively low level to a very high one. To the level of "Sketches by Boz" he never afterwards descended. To the level of "The Pickwick Papers" it is doubtful if he ever afterwards rose. "Pickwick," indeed, is not a good novel; but it is not a bad novel, for it is not a novel at all. In one sense, indeed, it is something nobler than a novel, for no novel with a plot and a proper termination could emit that sense of everlasting youth—a sense as of the gods gone wandering in England. This is not a novel, for all novels have an end; and "Pickwick," properly speaking, has no end—he is equal unto the angels. The point at which, as a fact, we find the printed matter terminates is not an end in any artistic sense of the word. Even as a boy I believed there were some more pages that were torn out of my copy, and I am looking for them still. The book might have been cut short anywhere else. It might have been cut short after Mr. Pickwick was released by Mr. Nupkins, or after Mr. Pickwick was fished out of the water, or at a hundred other places. And we should still have known that this was not really the story's end. We should have known that Mr. Pickwick was still having the same high adventures on the same high roads. As it happens, the book ends after Mr. Pickwick has taken a house in the neighbourhood of Dulwich. But we know he did not stop there. We know he broke out, that he took again the road of the high adventures; we know that if we take it ourselves in any acre of England, we may come suddenly upon him in a lane.

But this relation of "Pickwick" to the strict form of fiction demands a further word, which should indeed be said in any case before the consideration of any or all of the Dickens tales. Dickens's work is not to be reckoned in novels at all. Dickens's work is to be reckoned always by characters, sometimes by groups, oftener by episodes, but never by novels. You cannot discuss whether "Nicholas Nickleby" is a good novel, or whether "Our Mutual Friend" is a bad novel. Strictly, there is no such novel as "Nicholas Nickleby." There is no such novel as "Our Mutual Friend." They are simply lengths cut from the flowing and mixed substance called Dickens—a substance of which any given length will be certain to contain a given proportion of brilliant and of bad stuff. You can say, according to your opinions, "the Crummles part is perfect," or "the Boffins are a mistake," just as a man watching a river go by him could count here a floating flower, and there a streak of scum. But you cannot artistically divide the output into books. The best of his work can be found in the worst of his works. "A Tale of Two Cities" is a good novel; "Little Dorrit" is not a good novel. But the description of "The Circumlocution Office" in "Little Dorrit" is quite as good as the description of "Tellson's Bank" in "A Tale of Two Cities." "The Old Curiosity Shop" is not so good as "David Copperfield," but Swiveller is quite as good as Micawber. Nor is there any reason why these superb creatures, as a general rule, should be in one novel any more than another. There is no reason why Sam Weller, in the course of his wanderings, should not wander into "Nicholas Nickleby." There is no reason why Major Bagstock, in his brisk way, should not walk straight out of "Dombey and Son" and straight into "Martin Chuzzlewit." To this generalization some modification should be added. "Pickwick" stands by itself, and has even a sort of unity in not pretending to unity. "David Copperfield," in a less degree, stands by itself, as being the only book in which Dickens wrote of himself; and "A Tale of Two Cities" stands by itself as being the only book in which Dickens slightly altered himself. But as a whole, this should be firmly grasped, that the units of Dickens, the primary elements, are not the stories, but the characters who affect the stories—or, more often still, the characters who do not affect the stories.

This is a plain matter; but, unless it be stated and felt, Dickens may be greatly misunderstood and greatly underrated. For not only is his whole machinery directed to facilitating the self-display of certain characters, but something more deep and more unmodern still is also true of him. It is also true that all the *moving* machinery exists only to display entirely *static* character. Things in the Dickens story shift and change only in order to give us glimpses of great characters that do not change at all. If we had a sequel of Pickwick ten years afterwards, Pickwick would be exactly the same age. We know he would not have fallen into that strange and beautiful second childhood which soothed and simplified the end of Colonel Newcome. Newcome, throughout the book, is in an atmosphere of time: Pickwick, throughout the book, is not. This will probably be taken by most modern people as praise of Thackeray and dispraise of Dickens. But this only shows how few modern people understand Dickens. It also shows how few understand the faiths and the fables of mankind. The matter can only be roughly stated in one way. Dickens did not strictly make a literature; he made a mythology.

For a few years our corner of Western Europe has had a fancy for this thing we call fiction; that is, for writing down our own lives or similar lives in order to look at them. But though we call it fiction, it differs from older literatures chiefly in being less fictitious. It imitates not

only life, but the limitations of life; it not only reproduces life, it reproduces death. But outside us, in every
other country, in every other age, there has been going
on from the beginning a more fictitious kind of fiction.
I mean the kind now called folklore, the literature of
the people. Our modern novels, which deal with men as
they are, are chiefly produced by a small and educated
section of the society. But this other literature deals
with men greater than they are—with demi-gods and
heroes; and that is far too important a matter to be
trusted to the educated classes. The fashioning of these
portents is a popular trade, like ploughing or brick-
laying; the men who made hedges, the men who made
ditches, were the men who made deities. Men could not
elect their kings, but they could elect their gods. So we
find ourselves faced with a fundamental contrast between what is called fiction and what is called folklore.
The one exhibits an abnormal degree of dexterity oper-
ating within our daily limitations; the other exhibits
quite normal desires extended beyond those limitations.
Fiction means the common things as seen by the uncommon people. Fairy tales mean the uncommon things as
seen by the common people.

As our world advances through history towards its
present epoch, it becomes more specialist, less democratic, and folklore turns gradually into fiction. But it is
only slowly that the old elfin fire fades into the light of
common realism. For ages after our characters have
dressed up in the clothes of mortals they betray the
blood of the gods. Even our phraseology is full of relics
of this. When a modern novel is devoted to the bewilderments of a weak young clerk who cannot decide
which woman he wants to marry, or which new religion
he believes in, we still give this knock-kneed cad the
name of "the hero"—the name which is the crown of

Achilles. The popular preference for a story with "a happy ending" is not, or at least was not, a mere sweet-stuff optimism; it is the remains of the old idea of the triumph of the dragon-slayer, the ultimate apotheosis of the man beloved of heaven.

But there is another and more intangible trace of this fading supernaturalism—a trace very vivid to the reader, but very elusive to the critic. It is a certain air of end-lessness in the episodes, even in the shortest episodes—a sense that, although we leave them, they still go on. Our modern attraction to short stories is not an accident of form; it is the sign of a real sense of fleetingness and fragility; it means that existence is only an impression, and, perhaps, only an illusion. A short story of to-day has the air of a dream; it has the irrevocable beauty of a falsehood; we get a glimpse of grey streets of London or red plains of India, as in an opium vision; we see peo-ple—arresting people, with fiery and appealing faces. But when the story is ended, the people are ended. We have no instinct of anything ultimate and enduring be-hind the episodes. The moderns, in a word, describe life in short stories because they are possessed with the sen-timent that life itself is an uncommonly short story, and perhaps not a true one. But in this elder literature, even in the comic literature (indeed, especially in the comic literature), the reverse is true. The characters are felt to be fixed things of which we have fleeting glimpses; that is, they are felt to be divine. Uncle Toby is talking for ever, as the elves are dancing for ever. We feel that whenever we hammer on the house of Falstaff, Falstaff will be at home. We feel it as a Pagan would feel that, if a cry broke the silence after ages of unbelief, Apollo would still be listening in his temple. These writers may tell short stories, but we feel they are only parts of a long story. And herein lies the peculiar significance, the peculiar sacredness even, of penny dreadfuls and the common printed matter made for our errand-boys. Here in dim and desperate forms, under the ban of our base culture, stormed at by silly magistrates, sneered at by silly schoolmasters—here is the old popular literature still popular; here is the unmistakable voluminousness, the thousand and one tales of Dick Deadshot, like the thousand and one tales of Robin Hood. Here is the splendid and static boy, the boy who remains a boy through a thousand volumes and a thousand years. Here in mean alleys and dim shops, shadowed and shamed by the police, mankind is still driving its dark trade in heroes. And elsewhere, and in all other ages, in braver fashion, under cleaner skies the same eternal tale-telling goes on, and the whole mortal world is a factory of immortals.

Dickens was a mythologist rather than a novelist; he was the last of the mythologists, and perhaps the greatest. He did not always manage to make his characters men, but he always managed, at the least, to make them gods. They are creatures like Punch or Father Christmas. They live statically, in a perpetual summer of being themselves. It was not the aim of Dickens to show the effect of time and circumstance upon a character; it was not even his aim to show the effect of a character on time and circumstance. It is worth remark, in passing, that whenever he tried to describe change in a character, he made a mess of it, as in the repentance of Dombey or the apparent deterioration of Boffin. It was his aim to show character hung in a kind of happy void, in a world apart from time—yes, and essentially apart from circumstance, though the phrase may seem odd in connection with the godlike horse-play of "Pickwick." But all the Pickwickian events, wild as they often are, were only designed to display the greater wildness of souls, or sometimes merely to bring the reader within touch, so to speak, of that wildness. The author would have fired Mr. Pickwick out of a cannon to get him to Wardle's by Christmas; he would have taken the roof off to drop him into Bob Sawyer's party. But once put Pickwick at Wardle's, with his punch and a group of gorgeous personalities, and nothing will move him from his chair. Once he is at Sawyer's party, he forgets how he got there; he forgets Mrs. Bardell and all his story. For the story was but an incantation to call up a god, and the god (Mr. Jack Hopkins) is present in divine power. Once the great characters are face to face, the ladder by which they climbed is forgotten and falls down, the structure of the story drops to pieces, the plot is abandoned, the other characters deserted at every kind of crisis; the whole crowded thoroughfare of the tale is blocked by two or three talkers, who take their immortal ease as if they were already in Paradise. For they do not exist for the story; the story exists for them; and they know it.

To every man alive, one must hope, it has in some manner happened that he has talked with his more fascinating friends round a table on some night when all the numerous personalities unfolded themselves like great tropical flowers. All fell into their parts as in some delightful impromptu play. Every man was more himself than he had ever been in this vale of tears. Every man was a beautiful caricature of himself. The man who has known such nights will understand the exaggerations of "Pickwick." The man who has not known such nights will not enjoy "Pickwick" nor (I imagine) heaven. For, as I have said, Dickens is, in this matter, close to popular religion, which is the ultimate and reliable religion. He conceives an endless joy; he conceives creatures as permanent as Puck or Pan—creatures whose will to live æons upon æons cannot satisfy. He is not come, as a writer, that his creatures may copy life and copy its narrowness; he is come that they may have life, and that they may have it more abundantly. It is absurd indeed that Christians should be called the enemies of life because they wish life to last for ever; it is more absurd still to call the old comic writers dull because they wished their unchanging characters to last for ever. Both popular religion, with its endless joys, and the old comic story, with its endless jokes, have in our time faded together. We are too weak to desire that undying vigour. We believe that you can have too much of a good thing—a blasphemous belief, which at one blow wrecks all the heavens that men have hoped for. The grand old defiers of God were not afraid of an eternity of torment. We have come to be afraid of an eternity of joy. It is not my business here to take sides in this division between those who like life and long novels and those who like death and short stories; my only business is to point out that those who see in Dickens's unchanging characters and recurring catchwords a mere stiffness and lack of living movement miss the point and nature of his work. His tradition is another tradition altogether; his aim is another aim altogether to those of the modern novelists who trace the alchemy of experience and the autumn tints of character. He is there, like the common people of all ages, to make deities; he is there, as I have said, to exaggerate life in the direction of life. The spirit he at bottom celebrates is that of two friends drinking wine together and talking through the night. But for him they are two deathless friends talking through an endless night and pouring wine from an inexhaustible bottle.

This, then, is the first firm fact to grasp about "Pickwick"—about "Pickwick" more than about any of the other stories. It is, first and foremost, a supernatural story. Mr. Pickwick was a fairy. So was old Mr. Weller. This does not imply that they were suited to swing in a trapeze of gossamer; it merely implies that if they had fallen out of it on their heads they would not have died. But, to speak more strictly, Mr. Samuel Pickwick is not the fairy; he is the fairy prince; that is to say, he is the abstract wanderer and wonderer, the Ulysses of Comedy —the half-human and half-elfin creature—human enough to wander, human enough to wonder, but still sustained with that merry fatalism that is natural to immortal beings—sustained by that hint of divinity which tells him in the darkest hour that he is doomed to live happily ever afterwards. He has set out walking to the end of the world, but he knows he will find an inn there.

And this brings us to the best and boldest element of originality in "Pickwick." It has not, I think, been observed, and it may be that Dickens did not observe it. Certainly he did not plan it; it grew gradually, perhaps out of the unconscious part of his soul, and warmed the whole story like a slow fire. Of course it transformed the whole story also; transformed it out of all likeness to itself. About this latter point was waged one of the numberless little wars of Dickens. It was a part of his pugnacious vanity that he refused to admit the truth of the mildest criticism. Moreover, he used his inexhaustible ingenuity to find an apologia that was generally an afterthought. Instead of laughingly admitting, in answer to criticism, the glorious improbability of Pecksniff, he retorted with a sneer, clever and very unjust, that he was not surprised that the Pecksniffs should deny the portrait of Pecksniff. When it was objected that the pride of old Paul Dombey breaks as abruptly as a stick, he tried to make out that there had been an absorbing psychological struggle going on in that gentleman all the time, which the reader was too stupid to perceive.

Which is, I am afraid, rubbish. And so, in a similar vein, he answered those who pointed out to him the obvious and not very shocking fact that our sentiments about Pickwick are very different in the second part of the book from our sentiments in the first; that we find ourselves at the beginning setting out in the company of a farcical old fool, if not a farcical old humbug, and that we find ourselves at the end saying farewell to a fine old English merchant, a monument of genial sanity. Dickens answered with the same ingenious self-justification as in the other cases—that surely it often happened that a man met us first arrayed in his more grotesque qualities, and that fuller acquaintance unfolded his more serious merits. This, of course, is quite true; but I think any honest admirer of "Pickwick" will feel that it is not an answer. For the fault in "Pickwick" (if it be a fault) is a change, not in the hero but in the whole atmosphere. The point is not that Pickwick turns into a different kind of man; it is that "The Pickwick Papers" turns into a different kind of book. And however artistic both parts may be, this combination must, in strict art, be called inartistic. A man is quite artistically justified in writing a tale in which a man as cowardly as Bob Acres becomes a man as brave as Hector. But a man is not artistically justified in writing a tale which begins in the style of "The Rivals" and ends in the style of the "Iliad." In other words, we do not mind the hero changing in the course of a book; but we are not prepared for the author changing in the course of the book. And the author did change in the course of this book. He made, in the midst of this book, a great discovery, which was the discovery of his destiny, or, what is more important, of his duty. That discovery turned him from the author of "Sketches by Boz" to the author of "David Copperfield." And that discovery con-

68

stituted the thing of which I have spoken—the outstand-ing and arresting original feature in "The Pickwick Papers."

"Pickwick," I have said, is a romance of adventure, and Samuel Pickwick is the romantic adventurer. So much is indeed obvious. But the strange and stirring dis-covery which Dickens made was this—that having chosen a fat old man of the middle classes as a good thing of which to make a butt, he found that a fat old man of the middle classes is the very best thing of which to make a romantic adventurer. "Pickwick" is supremely original in that it is the adventures of an old man. It is a fairy tale in which the victor is not the youngest of the three brothers, but one of the oldest of their uncles. The result is both noble and new and true. There is nothing which so much needs simplicity as adventure. And there is no one who so much possesses simplicity as an honest and elderly man of business. For romance he is better than a troop of young troubadours; for the swaggering young fellow anticipates his adventures, just as he an-ticipates his income. Hence, both the adventures and the income, when he comes up to them, are not there. But a man in late middle-age has grown used to the plain necessities, and his first holiday is a second youth. A good man, as Thackeray said with such thorough and searching truth, grows simpler as he grows older. Sam-uel Pickwick in his youth was probably an insufferable young coxcomb. He knew then, or thought he knew, all about the confidence tricks of swindlers like Jingle. He knew then, or thought he knew, all about the amatory designs of sly ladies like Mrs. Bardell. But years and real life have relieved him of this idle and evil knowledge. He has had the high good luck in losing the follies of youth, to lose the wisdom of youth also. Dickens has caught, in a manner at once wild and convincing, this queer innocence of the afternoon of life. The round, moon-like face, the round, moon-like spectacles of Samuel Pickwick move through the tale as emblems of a certain spherical simplicity. They are fixed in that grave surprise that may be seen in babies; that grave surprise which is the only real happiness that is possible to man. Pickwick's round face is like a round and honourable mirror, in which are reflected all the fantasies of earthly existence; for surprise is, strictly speaking, the only kind of reflection. All this grew gradually on Dickens. It is odd to recall to our minds the original plan, the plan of the Nimrod Club, and the author who was to be wholly occupied in playing practical jokes on his characters. He had chosen (or somebody else had chosen) that corpulent old simpleton as a person peculiarly fitted to fall down trap-doors, to shoot over butter slides, to struggle with apple-pie beds, to be tipped out of carts and dipped into horse-ponds. But Dickens, and Dickens only, discovered as he went on how fitted the fat old man was to rescue ladies, to defy tyrants, to dance, to leap, to experiment with life, to be a *deus ex machinâ,* and even a knight-errant. Dickens made this discovery. Dickens went into the Pickwick Club to scoff, and Dickens remained to pray.

Molière and his marquises are very much amused when M. Jourdain, the fat old middle-class fellow, discovers with delight that he has been talking prose all his life. I have often wondered whether Molière saw how in this fact M. Jourdain towers above them all and touches the stars. He has the freshness to enjoy a fresh fact, the freshness to enjoy an old one. He can feel that the common thing prose is an accomplishment like verse; and it is an accomplishment like verse; it is the miracle of language. He can feel the subtle taste of water, and roll it on his tongue like wine. His simple vanity and voracity, his innocent love of living, his ignorant love of learning, are things far fuller of romance than the weariness and foppishness of the sniggering cavaliers. When he consciously speaks prose, he unconsciously thinks poetry. It would be better for us all if we were as conscious that supper is supper or that life is life, as this true romantic was that prose is actually prose. M. Jourdain is here the type, Mr. Pickwick is elsewhere the type, of this true and neglected thing, the romance of the middle classes. It is the custom in our little epoch to sneer at the middle classes. Cockney artists profess to find the bourgeoisie dull; as if artists had any business to find anything dull. Decadents talk contemptuously of its conventions and its set tasks; it never occurs to them that conventions and set tasks are the very way to keep that greenness in the grass and that redness in the roses —which they had lost for ever. Stevenson, in his incomparable "Lantern Bearers," describes the ecstasy of a schoolboy in the mere fact of buttoning a dark lantern under a dark great-coat. If you wish for that ecstasy of the schoolboy, you must have the boy; but you must also have the school. Strict opportunities and defined hours are the very outline of that enjoyment. A man like Mr. Pickwick has been at school all his life, and when he comes out he astonishes the youngsters. His heart, as that acute psychologist, Mr. Weller, points out, had been born later than his body. It will be remembered that Mr. Pickwick also, when on the escapade of Winkle and Miss Allen, took immoderate pleasure in the performances of a dark lantern which was not dark enough, and was nothing but a nuisance to everybody. His soul also was with Stevenson's boys on the grey sands of Haddington, talking in the dark by the sea. He also was of the league of the "Lantern Bearers." Stevenson, I remember, says that in the shops of that town they could purchase "penny Pickwicks (that remarkable cigar)." Let us hope they smoked them, and that the rotund ghost of Pickwick hovered over the rings of smoke.

Pickwick goes through life with that godlike gullibility which is the key to all adventures. The greenhorn is the ultimate victor in everything; it is he that gets the most out of life. Because Pickwick is led away by Jingle, he will be led to the White Hart Inn, and see the only Weller cleaning boots in the courtyard. Because he is bamboozled by Dodson and Fogg, he will enter the prison house like a paladin, and rescue the man and the woman who have wronged him most. His soul will never starve for exploits or excitements who is wise enough to be made a fool of. He will make himself happy in the traps that have been laid for him; he will roll in their nets and sleep. All doors will fly open to him who has a mildness more defiant than mere courage. The whole is unerringly expressed in one fortunate phrase—he will be always "taken in." To be taken in everywhere is to see the inside of everything. It is the hospitality of circumstance. With torches and trumpets, like a guest, the greenhorn is taken in by Life. And the sceptic is cast out by it.

CHAPTER V

The Great Popularity

THERE is one aspect of Charles Dickens which must be of interest even to that subterranean race which does not admire his books. Even if we are not interested in Dickens as a great event in English literature, we must still be interested in him as a great event in English history. If he had not his place with Fielding and Thackeray, he would still have his place with Wat Tyler and Wilkes; for the man led a mob. He did what no English statesman, perhaps, has really done; he called out the people. He was popular in a sense of which we moderns have not even a notion. In that sense there is no popularity now. There are no popular authors today. We call such authors as Mr. Guy Boothby or Mr. William Le Queux popular authors. But this is popularity altogether in a weaker sense; not only in quantity, but in quality. The old popularity was positive; the new is negative. There is a great deal of difference between the eager man who wants to read a book, and the tired man who wants a book to read. A man reading a Le Queux mystery wants to get to the end of it. A man reading the Dickens novel wished that it might never end. Men read a Dickens story six times because they knew it so well. If a man can read a Le Queux story six times it is only because he can forget it six times. In short, the Dickens novel was popular, not because it was an unreal world, but because it was a real world; a world in which the soul could live. The modern "shocker" at its very best is an interlude in life. But in the days when Dickens's work was coming out in serial, people talked as if real life were itself the interlude between one issue of "Pickwick" and another.

In reaching the period of the publication of "Pickwick," we reach this sudden apotheosis of Dickens. Henceforward he filled the literary world in a way hard to imagine. Fragments of that huge fashion remain in our daily language; in the talk of every trade or public question are embedded the wrecks of that enormous religion. Men give out the airs of Dickens without even opening his books; just as Catholics can live in a tradition of Christianity without having looked at the New Testament. The man in the street has more memories of Dickens, whom he has not read, than of Marie Corelli, whom he has. There is nothing in any way parallel to this omnipresence and vitality in the great comic characters of Boz. There are no modern Bumbles and Pecksniffs, no modern Gamps and Micawbers. Mr. Rudyard Kipling (to take an author of a higher type than those before mentioned) is called, and called justly, a popular author; that is to say, he is widely read, greatly enjoyed, and highly remunerated; he has achieved the paradox of at once making poetry and making money. But let any one who wishes to see the difference try the experiment of assuming the Kipling characters to be common property like the Dickens characters. Let any one go into an average parlour and allude to Strickland as he would allude to Mr. Bumble, the Beadle. Let any one say that somebody is "a perfect Learoyd," as he would say "a perfect Pecksniff." Let any one write a comic paragraph for a halfpenny paper, and allude to Mrs. Hawksbee instead of to Mrs. Gamp. He will soon discover that the modern world has forgotten its own fiercest booms more completely than it has forgotten this formless tradition from its fathers. The mere dregs of it come to more than any contemporary excitement; the gleaning of the grapes of "Pickwick" is more than the whole vintage of "Soldiers Three." There is one instance, and I think only one, of an exception to this generalization; there is one figure in our popular literature which would really be recognized by the populace. Ordinary men would understand you if you referred currently to Sherlock Holmes. Sir Arthur Conan Doyle would no doubt be justified in rearing his head to the stars, remembering that Sherlock Holmes is the only really familiar figure in modern fiction. But let him droop that head again with a gentle sadness, remembering that if Sherlock Holmes is the only familiar figure in modern fiction, Sherlock Holmes is also the only familiar figure in the Sherlock Holmes tales. Not many people could say offhand what was the name of the owner of Silver Blaze, or whether Mrs. Watson was dark or fair. But if Dickens had written the Sherlock Holmes stories, every character in them would have been equally arresting and memorable. A Sherlock Holmes would have cooked the dinner for Sherlock Holmes; a Sherlock Holmes would have driven his cab. If Dickens brought in a man merely to carry a letter, he had time for a touch or two, and made him a giant. Dickens not only conquered the world, he conquered it with minor characters. Mr. John Smauker, the servant of Mr. Cyrus Bantam, though he merely passes across the stage, is almost as vivid to us as Mr. Samuel Weller, the servant of Mr. Samuel Pickwick. The young man with the lumpy forehead, who only says

"Esker" to Mr. Podsnap's foreign gentleman, is as good as Mr. Podsnap himself. They appear only for a fragment of time, but they belong to eternity. We have them only for an instant, but they have us for ever.

In dealing with Dickens, then, we are dealing with a man whose public success was a marvel and almost a monstrosity. And here I perceive that my friend, the purely artistic critic, primed with Flaubert and Turgenev, can contain himself no longer. He leaps to his feet, upsetting his cup of cocoa, and asks contemptuously what all this has to do with criticism. "Why begin your study of an author," he says, "with trash about popularity? Boothby is popular, and Le Queux is popular, and Mother Siegel is popular. If Dickens was even more popular, it may only mean that Dickens was even worse. The people like bad literature. If your object is to show that Dickens was good literature, you should rather apologize for his popularity, and try to explain it away. You should seek to show that Dickens's work was good literature, although it was popular. Yes, that is your task, to prove that Dickens was admirable, although he was admired!"

I ask the artistic critic to be patient for a little and to believe that I have a serious reason for registering this historic popularity. To that we shall come presently. But as a manner of approach I may perhaps ask leave to examine this actual and fashionable statement, to which I have supposed him to have recourse—the statement that the people like bad literature, and even like literature because it is bad. This way of stating the thing is an error, and in that error lies matter of much import to Dickens and his destiny in letters. The public does not like bad literature. The public likes a certain kind of literature and likes that kind of literature even when it is bad better than another kind of literature even

76

when it is good. Nor is this unreasonable; for the line between different types of literature is as real as the line between tears and laughter; and to tell people who can only get bad comedy that you have some first-class tragedy is as irrational as to offer a man who is shivering over weak warm coffee a really superior sort of ice.

Ordinary people dislike the delicate modern work, not because it is good or because it is bad, but because it is not the thing that they asked for. If, for instance, you find them pent in sterile streets and hungering for adventure and a violent secrecy, and if you then give them their choice between "A Study in Scarlet," a good detective story, and "The Autobiography of Mark Rutherford," a good psychological monologue, no doubt they will prefer "A Study in Scarlet." But they will not do so because "The Autobiography of Mark Rutherford" is a very good monologue, but because it is evidently a very poor detective story. They will be indifferent to "Les Aveugles," not because it is good drama, but because it is bad melodrama. They do not like good introspective sonnets; but neither do they like bad introspective sonnets, of which there are many. When they walk behind the brass of the Salvation Army band instead of listening to harmonies at Queen's Hall, it is always assumed that they prefer bad music. But it may be merely that they prefer military music, music marching down the open street, and that if Dan Godfrey's band could be smitten with salvation and lead them, they would like that even better. And while they might easily get more satisfaction out of a screaming article in *The War Cry* than out of a page of Emerson about the Oversoul, this would not be because the page of Emerson is another and superior kind of literature. It would be because the page of Emerson is another (and inferior) kind of religion.

77

Dickens stands first as a defiant monument of what happens when a great literary genius has a literary taste akin to that of the community. For this kinship was deep and spiritual. Dickens was not like our ordinary demagogues and journalists. Dickens did not write what the people wanted. Dickens wanted what the people wanted. And with this was connected that other fact which must never be forgotten, and which I have more than once insisted on, that Dickens and his school had a hilarious faith in democracy and thought of the service of it as a sacred priesthood. Hence there was this vital point in his popularism, that there was no condescension in it. The belief that the rabble will only read rubbish can be read between the lines of all our contemporary writers, even of those writers whose rubbish the rabble reads. Mr. Fergus Hume has no more respect for the populace than Mr. George Moore. The only difference lies between those writers who will consent to talk down to the people, and those writers who will not consent to talk down to the people. But Dickens never talked down to the people. He talked up to the people. He approached the people like a deity and poured out his riches and his blood. This is what makes the immortal bond between him and the masses of men. He had not merely produced something they could understand, but he took it seriously, and toiled and agonized to produce it. They were not only enjoying one of the best writers, they were enjoying the best he could do. His raging and sleepless nights, his wild walks in the darkness, his note-books crowded, his nerves in rags, all this extraordinary output was but a fit sacrifice to the ordinary man. He climbed towards the lower classes. He panted upwards on weary wings to reach the heaven of the poor.

His power, then, lay in the fact that he expressed with

78

an energy and brilliancy quite uncommon the things close to the common mind. But with this mere phrase, the common mind, we collide with a current error. Commonness and the common mind are now generally spoken of as meaning in some manner inferiority and the inferior mind; the mind of the mere mob. But the common mind means the mind of all the artists and heroes; or else it would not be common. Plato had the common mind; Dante had the common mind; or that mind was not common. Commonness means the quality common to the saint and the sinner, to the philosopher and the fool; and it was this that Dickens grasped and developed. In everybody there is a certain thing that loves babies, that fears death, that likes sunlight: that thing enjoys Dickens. And everybody does not mean uneducated crowds; everybody means everybody: everybody means Mrs. Meynell. This lady, a cloistered and fastidious writer, has written one of the best eulogies of Dickens that exist, an essay in praise of his pungent perfection of epithet. And when I say that everybody understands Dickens I do not mean that he is suited to the untaught intelligence. I mean that he is so plain that even scholars can understand him.

The best expression of the fact, however, is to be found in noting the two things in which he is most triumphant. In order of artistic value, next after his humour, comes his horror. And both his humour and his horror are of a kind strictly to be called human; that is, they belong to the basic part of us, below the lowest roots of our variety. His horror for instance is a healthy churchyard horror, a fear of the grotesque defamation called death; and this every man has, even if he also has the more delicate and depraved fears that come of an evil spiritual outlook. We may be afraid of a fine shade with Henry James; that is, we may be afraid of the

world. We may be afraid of a taut silence with Maeterlinck; that is, we may be afraid of our own souls. But
every one will certainly be afraid of a Cock Lane Ghost,
including Henry James and Maeterlinck. This latter is
literally a mortal fear, a fear of death; it is not the immortal fear, or fear of damnation, which belongs to all
the more refined intellects of our day. In a word, Dickens does, in the exact sense, make the flesh creep; he
does not, like the decadents, make the soul crawl. And
the creeping of the flesh on being reminded of its fleshly
failure is a strictly universal thing which we can all feel,
while some of us are as yet uninstructed in the art of
spiritual crawling. In the same way the Dickens mirth
is a part of man and universal. All men can laugh at
broad humour, even the subtle humourists. Even the
modern *flâneur,* who can smile at a particular combination of green and yellow, would laugh at Mr. Lammle's
request for Mr. Fledgeby's nose. In a word—the common
things are common—even to the uncommon people.

These two primary dispositions of Dickens, to make
the flesh creep and to make the sides ache, were a sort of
twins of his spirit; they were never far apart and the fact
of their affinity is interestingly exhibited in the first two
novels.

Generally he mixed the two up in a book and mixed
a great many other things with them. As a rule he cared
little if he kept six stories of quite different colours running in the same book. The effect was sometimes similar
to that of playing six tunes at once. He does not mind
the coarse tragic figure of Jonas Chuzzlewit crossing the
mental stage which is full of the allegorical pantomime
of Eden, Mr. Chollop and *The Watertoast Gazette,* a
scene which is as much of a satire as "Gulliver," and
nearly as much of a fairy tale. He does not mind bind-
ing up a rather pompous sketch of prostitution in the

same book with an adorable impossibility like Bunsby. But "Pickwick" is so far a coherent thing that it is coherently comic and consistently rambling. And as a consequence his next book was, upon the whole, coherently and consistently horrible. As his natural turn for terrors was kept down in "Pickwick," so his natural turn for joy and laughter is kept down in "Oliver Twist." In "Oliver Twist" the smoke of the thieves' kitchen hangs over the whole tale, and the shadow of Fagin falls everywhere. The little lamp-lit rooms of Mr. Brownlow and Rose Maylie are to all appearance purposely kept subordinate, a mere foil to the foul darkness without. It was a strange and appropriate accident that Cruikshank and not "Phiz" should have illustrated this book. There was about Cruikshank's art a kind of cramped energy which is almost the definition of the criminal mind. His drawings have a dark strength: yet he does not only draw morbidly, he draws meanly. In the doubled-up figure and frightful eyes of Fagin in the condemned cell there is not only a baseness of subject; there is a kind of baseness in the very technique of it. It is not drawn with the free lines of a free man; it has the half-witted secrecies of a hunted thief. It does not look merely like a picture of Fagin; it looks like a picture by Fagin. Among these dark and detestable plates there is one which has with a kind of black directness, the dreadful poetry that does inhere in the story, stumbling as it often is. It represents Oliver asleep at an open window in the house of one of his humaner patrons. And outside the window, but as big and close as if they were in the room, stand Fagin and the foul-faced Monk, staring at him with dark monstrous visages and great, white wicked eyes, in the style of the simple deviltry of the draughtsman. The very *naïveté* of the horror is horrifying: the very woodenness of the two wicked men seems to make them worse than mere men who are wicked. But this picture of big devils at the window-sill does express, as has been suggested above, the thread of poetry in the whole thing; the sense, that is, of the thieves as a kind of army of devils compassing earth and sky, crying for Oliver's soul and besieging the house in which he is barred for safety. In this matter there is, I think, a difference between the author and the illustrator. In Cruikshank there was surely something morbid; but, sensitive and sentimental as Dickens was, there was nothing morbid in him. He had, as Stevenson had, more of the mere boy's love of suffocating stories of blood and darkness; of skulls, of gibbets, of all the things, in a word, that are sombre without being sad. There is a ghastly joy in remembering our boyish reading about Sikes and his flight; especially about the voice of that unbearable pedlar which went on in a monotonous and maddening sing-song, "will wash out grease-stains, mud-stains, blood-stains," until Sikes fled almost screaming. For this boyish mixture of appetite and repugnance there is a good popular phrase, "supping on horrors." Dickens supped on horrors as he supped on Christmas pudding. He supped on horrors because he was an optimist and could sup on anything. There was no saner or simpler schoolboy than Traddles, who covered all his books with skeletons.

"Oliver Twist" had begun in Bentley's *Miscellany*, which Dickens edited in 1837. It was interrupted by a blow that for the moment broke the author's spirit and seemed to have broken his heart. His wife's sister, Mary Hogarth, died suddenly. To Dickens his wife's family seems to have been like his own; his affections were heavily committed to the sisters, and of this one he was peculiarly fond. All his life, through much conceit and sometimes something bordering on selfishness, we can feel the redeeming note of an almost tragic tenderness; he was a man who could really have died of love or sorrow. He took up the work of "Oliver Twist" again later in the year, and finished it at the end of 1838. His work was incessant and almost bewildering. In 1838 he had already brought out the first number of "Nicholas Nickleby." But the great popularity went booming on; the whole world was roaring for books by Dickens, and more books by Dickens, and Dickens was labouring night and day like a factory. Among other things he edited the "Memoirs of Grimaldi." The incident is only worth mentioning for the sake of one more example of the silly ease with which Dickens was drawn by criticism and the clever ease with which he managed, in these small squabbles, to defend himself. Somebody mildly suggested that, after all, Dickens had never known Grimaldi. Dickens was down on him like a thunderbolt, sardonically asking how close an intimacy Lord Braybrooke had with Mr. Samuel Pepys.

"Nicholas Nickleby" is the most typical perhaps of the tone of his earlier works. It is in form a very rambling, old-fashioned romance, the kind of romance in which the hero is only a convenience for the frustration of the villain. Nicholas is what is called in theatricals a stick. But any stick is good enough to beat a Squeers with. That strong thwack, that simplified energy is the whole object of such a story; and the whole of this tale is full of a kind of highly picturesque platitude. The wicked aristocrats, Sir Mulberry Hawk, Lord Frederick Verisopht and the rest are inadequate versions of the fashionable profligate. But this is not (as some suppose) because Dickens in his vulgarity could not comprehend the refinement of patrician vice. There is no idea more vulgar or more ignorant than the notion that a gentleman is generally what is called refined. The error of the Hawk conception is that, if anything, he is too refined. Real aristocratic blackguards do not swagger and rant so well. A real fast baronet would not have defied Nicholas in the tavern with so much oratorical dignity. A real fast baronet would probably have been choked with apoplectic embarrassment and said nothing at all. But Dickens read into this aristocracy a grandiloquence and a natural poetry which, like all melodrama, is really the precious jewel of the poor.

But the book contains something which is much more Dickensian. It is exquisitely characteristic of Dickens that the truly great achievement of the story is the person who delays the story. Mrs. Nickleby with her beautiful mazes of memory does her best to prevent the story of Nicholas Nickleby from being told. And she does well. There is no particular necessity that we should know what happens to Madeline Bray. There is a desperate and crying necessity that we should know that Mrs. Nickleby once had a foot-boy who had a wart on his nose and a driver who had a green shade over his left eye. If Mrs. Nickleby is a fool, she is one of those fools who are wiser than the world. She stands for a great truth which we must not forget; the truth that experience is not in real life a saddening thing at all. The people who have had misfortunes are generally the people who love to talk about them. Experience is really one of the gaieties of old age, one of its dissipations. Mere memory becomes a kind of debauch. Experience may be disheartening to those who are foolish enough to try to co-ordinate it and to draw deductions from it. But to those happy souls, like Mrs. Nickleby, to whom relevancy is nothing, the whole of their past life is like an inexhaustible fairyland. Just as we take a rambling walk because we know that a whole district is beautiful, so they indulge a rambling mind because they know that a whole existence is interesting. A boy does not plunge into his future more romantically and at random, than they plunge into their past.

Another gleam in the book is Mr. Mantalini. Of him, as of all the really great comic characters of Dickens, it is impossible to speak with any critical adequacy. Perfect absurdity is a direct thing, like physical pain, or a strong smell. A joke is a fact. However indefensible it is it cannot be attacked. However defensible it is it cannot be defended. That Mr. Mantalini should say in praising the "outline" of his wife, "The two Countesses had no outlines, and the Dowager's was a demd outline," this can only be called an unanswerable absurdity. You may try to analyze it, as Charles Lamb did the indefensible joke about the hare; you may dwell for a moment on the dark distinctions between the negative disqualification of the Countesses and the positive disqualification of the Dowager, but you will not capture the violent beauty of it in any way. "She will be a lovely widow; I shall be a body. Some handsome women will cry; she will laugh demnedly." This vision of demoniac heartlessness has the same defiant finality. I mention the matter here, but it has to be remembered in connection with all the comic masterpieces of Dickens. Dickens has greatly suffered with the critics precisely through this stunning simplicity in his best work. The critic is called upon to describe his sensations while enjoying Mantalini and Micawber, and he can no more describe them than he can describe a blow in the face. Thus Dickens, in this self-conscious, analytical and descriptive age, loses both ways. He is doubly unfitted for the best modern criticism. His bad work is below that criticism. His good work is above it.

But gigantic as were Dickens's labours, gigantic as were the exactions from him, his own plans were more gigantic still. He had the type of mind that wishes to do every kind of work at once; to do everybody's work as well as its own. There floated before him a vision of a monstrous magazine, entirely written by himself. It is true that when this scheme came to be discussed, he suggested that other pens might be occasionally employed; but, reading between the lines, it is sufficiently evident that he thought of the thing as a kind of vast multiplication of himself, with Dickens as editor, opening letters, Dickens as leader-writer writing leaders, Dickens as reporter reporting meetings, Dickens as reviewer reviewing books, Dickens, for all I know, as office-boy, opening and shutting doors. This serial, of which he spoke to Messrs. Chapman and Hall, began and broke off and remains as a colossal fragment bound together under the title of "Master Humphrey's Clock." One characteristic thing he wished to have in the periodical. He suggested an Arabian Nights of London, in which Gog and Magog, the giants of the city, should give forth chronicles as enormous as themselves. He had a taste for these schemes or frameworks for many tales. He made and abandoned many; many he half-fulfilled. I strongly suspect that he meant Major Jackman, in "Mrs. Lirriper's Lodgings" and "Mrs. Lirriper's Legacy," to start a series of studies of that lady's lodgers, a kind of history of No. 81 Norfolk Street, Strand. "The Seven Poor Travellers" was planned for seven stories; we will not say seven poor stories. Dickens had meant, probably, to write a tale for each article of "Somebody's Luggage": he only got as far as the hat and the boots. This gigantesque scale of literary architecture, huge and yet curiously cosy, is characteristic of his spirit, fond of size and yet fond of comfort. He liked to have story within story, like room within room of some labyrinthine but comfortable castle. In this spirit he wished "Master Hum-

phrey's Clock" to begin, and to be a big frame or book-
case for numberless novels. The clock started; but the
clock stopped.

In the prologue by Master Humphrey reappear Mr.
Pickwick and Sam Weller, and of that resurrection
many things have been said, chiefly expressions of a
reasonable regret. Doubtless they do not add much to
their author's reputation, but they add a great deal to
their author's pleasure. It was ingrained in him to wish
to meet old friends. All his characters are, so to speak,
designed to be old friends; in a sense every Dickens
character is an old friend, even when he first appears.
He comes to us mellow out of many implied interviews,
and carries the firelight on his face. Dickens was simply
pleased to meet Pickwick again, and being pleased, he
made the old man too comfortable to be amusing.

But "Master Humphrey's Clock" is now scarcely
known except as the shell of one of the well-known
novels. "The Old Curiosity Shop" was published in accordance with the original "Clock" scheme. Perhaps
the most typical thing about it is the title. There seems
no reason in particular, at the first and most literal
glance, why the story should be called after the Old
Curiosity Shop. Only two of the characters have anything to do with such a shop, and they leave us for ever
in the first few pages. It is as if Thackeray had called
the whole novel of "Vanity Fair" "Miss Pinkerton's
Academy." It is as if Scott had given the whole story of
"The Antiquary" the title of "The Hawes Inn." But
when we feel the situation with more fidelity we realize
that this title is something in the nature of a key to the
whole Dickens romance. His tales always started from
some splendid hint in the streets. And shops, perhaps
the most poetical of all things, often set off his fancy
galloping. Every shop, in fact, was to him the door of

romance. Among all the huge serial schemes of which we have spoken, it is a matter of wonder that he never started an endless periodical called "The Street," and divided it into shops. He could have written an exquisite romance called "The Baker's Shop"; another called "The Chemist's Shop"; another called "The Oil Shop," to keep company with "The Old Curiosity Shop." Some incomparable baker he invented and forgot. Some gorgeous chemist might have been. Some more than mortal oilman is lost to us for ever. This Old Curiosity Shop he did happen to linger by: its tale he did happen to tell.

Around "Little Nell," of course, a controversy raged and rages; some implored Dickens not to kill her at the end of the story: some regret that he did not kill her at the beginning. To me the chief interest in this young person lies in the fact that she is an example, and the most celebrated example of what must have been, I think, a personal peculiarity, perhaps a personal experience of Dickens. There is, of course, no paradox at all in saying that if we find in a good book a wildly impossible character it is very probable indeed that it was copied from a real person. This is one of the commonplaces of good art criticism. For although people talk of the restraints of fact and the freedom of fiction, the case for most artistic purposes is quite the other way. Nature is as free as air: art is forced to look probable. There may be a million things that do happen, and yet only one thing that convinces us as likely to happen. Out of a million possible things there may be only one appropriate thing. I fancy, therefore, that many stiff, unconvincing characters are copied from the wild freak-show of real life. And in many parts of Dickens's work there is evidence of some peculiar affection on his part for a strange sort of little girl; a little girl with a premature sense of responsibility and duty; a sort of saintly precocity. Did he know some little girl of this kind? Did she die, perhaps, and remain in his memory in colours too ethereal and pale? In any case there are a great number of them in his works. Little Dorrit was one of them, and Florence Dombey with her brother, and even Agnes in infancy; and, of course, Little Nell. And, in any case, one thing is evident; whatever charm these children may have they have not the charm of childhood. They are not little children: they are "little mothers." The beauty and divinity in a child lie in his not being worried, not being conscientious, not being like Little Nell. Little Nell has never any of the sacred bewilderment of a baby. She never wears that face, beautiful but almost half-witted, with which a real child half understands that there is evil in the universe.

As usual, however, little as the story has to do with the title, the splendid and satisfying pages have even less to do with the story. Dick Swiveller is perhaps the noblest of all the noble creations of Dickens. He has all the overwhelming absurdity of Mantalini, with the addition of being human and credible, for he knows he is absurd. His high-falutin is not done because he seriously thinks it right and proper, like that of Mr. Snodgrass, nor is it done because he thinks it will serve his turn, like that of Mr. Pecksniff, for both these beliefs are improbable; it is done because he really loves high-falutin, because he has a lonely literary pleasure in exaggerative language. Great draughts of words are to him like great draughts of wine—pungent and yet refreshing, light and yet leaving him in a glow. In unerring instinct for the perfect folly of a phrase he has no equal, even among the giants of Dickens. "I am sure," says Miss Wackles, when she had been flirting with Cheggs, the market-gardener, and reduced Mr.

Swiveller to Byronic renunciation, "I am sure I'm very sorry if—" "Sorry," said Mr. Swiveller, "sorry in the possession of a Cheggs!" The abyss of bitterness is unfathomable. Scarcely less precious is the pose of Mr. Swiveller when he imitates the stage brigand. After crying, "Some wine here! Ho!" he hands the flagon to himself with profound humility, and receives it haughtily. Perhaps the very best scene in the book is that between Mr. Swiveller and the single gentleman with whom he endeavours to remonstrate for having remained in bed all day: "We cannot have single gentlemen coming into the place and sleeping like double gentlemen without paying extra. . . . An equal amount of slumber was never got out of one bed, and if you want to sleep like that you must pay for a double-bedded room." His relations with the Marchioness are at once purely romantic and purely genuine; there is nothing even of Dickens's legitimate exaggerations about them. A shabby, larky, good-natured clerk would, as a matter of fact, spend hours in the society of a little servant girl if he found her about the house. It would arise partly from a dim kindliness, and partly from that mysterious instinct which is sometimes called, mistakenly, a love of low company—that mysterious instinct which makes so many men of pleasure find something soothing in the society of uneducated people, particularly uneducated women. It is the instinct which accounts for the otherwise unaccountable popularity of barmaids.

And still the pot of that huge popularity boiled. In 1841 another novel was demanded, and "Barnaby Rudge" supplied. It is chiefly of interest as an embodiment of that other element in Dickens, the picturesque or even the pictorial. Barnaby Rudge, the idiot with his rags and his feathers and his raven, the bestial hangman, the blind mob—all make a picture, though they hardly make a novel. One touch there is in it of the richer and more humorous Dickens, the boy-conspirator, Mr. Sim Tappertit. But he might have been treated with more sympathy—with as much sympathy, for instance, as Mr. Dick Swiveller; for he is only the romantic guttersnipe, the bright boy at the particular age when it is most fascinating to found a secret society and most difficult to keep a secret. And if ever there was a romantic guttersnipe on earth it was Charles Dickens. "Barnaby Rudge" is no more an historical novel than Sim's secret league was a political movement; but they are both beautiful creations. When all is said, however, the main reason for mentioning the work here is that it is the next bubble in the pot, the next thing that burst out of that whirling, seething head. The tide of it rose and smoked and sang till it boiled over the pot of Britain and poured over all America. In the January of 1842 he set out for the United States.

CHAPTER VI

Dickens and America

THE essential of Dickens's character was the conjunction of common sense with uncommon sensibility. The two things are not, indeed, in such an antithesis as is commonly imagined. Great English literary authorities, such as Jane Austen and Mr. Chamberlain, have put the word "sense" and the word "sensibility" in a kind of opposition to each other. But not only are they not opposite words: they are actually the same word. They both mean receptiveness or approachability by the facts outside us. To have a sense of colour is the same as to have a sensibility to colour. A person who realizes that beef-steaks are appetizing shows his sensibility. A person who realizes that moonrise is romantic shows his sense. But it is not difficult to see the meaning and need of the popular distinction between sensibility and sense, particularly in the form called common sense. Common sense is a sensibility duly distributed in all normal directions; sensibility has come to mean a specialized sensibility in one. This is unfortunate, for it is not the sensibility that is bad, but the specializing; that is, the lack of sensibility to everything else. A young lady who stays out all night to look at the stars should not be blamed for her sensibility to starlight, but for her insensibility to other people. A poet who recites his own verses from ten to five with the tears rolling down his face should decidedly be rebuked for his lack of sensibility—his lack of sensibility to those grand rhythms of the social harmony, crudely called manners. For all politeness is a long poem, since it is full of recurrences. This balance of all the sensibilities we call sense; and it is in this capacity that it becomes of great importance as an attribute of the character of Dickens.

Dickens, I repeat, had common sense and uncommon sensibility. That is to say, the proportion of interests in him was about the same as that of an ordinary man, but he felt all of them more excitedly. This is a distinction not easy for us to keep in mind, because we hear to-day chiefly of two types, the dull man who likes ordinary things mildly, and the extraordinary man who likes extraordinary things wildly. But Dickens liked quite ordinary things; he merely made an extraordinary fuss about them. His excitement was sometimes like an epileptic fit; but it must not be confused with the fury of the man of one idea or one line of ideas. He had the excess of the eccentric, but not the defects, the narrowness. Even when he raved like a maniac he did not rave like a monomaniac. He had no particular spot of sensibility or spot of insensibility: he was merely a normal man minus a normal self-command. He had no special point of mental pain or repugnance, like Ruskin's horror of steam and iron, or Mr. Bernard Shaw's permanent irritation against romantic love. He was annoyed at the ordinary annoyances: only he was more annoyed than was necessary. He did not desire strange delights, blue wine or black women with Baudelaire, or cruel sights east of Suez with Mr. Kipling. He wanted what a healthy man wants, only he was ill with wanting it. To under-

93

stand him, in a word, we must keep well in mind the medical distinction between delicacy and disease. Perhaps we shall comprehend it and him more clearly if we think of a woman rather than a man. There was much that was feminine about Dickens, and nothing more so than this abnormal normality. A woman is often, in comparison with a man, at once more sensitive and more sane.

This distinction must be especially remembered in all his quarrels. And it must be most especially remembered in what may be called his great quarrel with America, which we have now to approach. The whole matter is so typical of Dickens's attitude to everything and anything, and especially of Dickens's attitude to anything political, that I may ask permission to approach the matter by another, a somewhat long and curving avenue.

Common sense is a fairy thread, thin and faint, and as easily lost as gossamer. Dickens (in large matters) never lost it. Take, as an example, his political tone or drift throughout his life. His views, of course, may have been right or wrong; the reforms he supported may have been successful or otherwise: that is not a matter for this book. But if we compare him with the other men that wanted the same things (or the other men that wanted the other things) we feel a startling absence of cant, a startling sense of humanity as it is, and of the eternal weakness. He was a fierce democrat, but in his best vein he laughed at the cocksure Radical of common life, the red-faced man who said, "Prove it!" when anybody said anything. He fought for the right to elect; but he would not whitewash elections. He believed in parliamentary government; but he did not, like our contemporary newspapers, pretend that parliament is something much more heroic and imposing than it is. He fought for the rights of the grossly oppressed Nonconformists; but he spat out of his mouth the unction of that too easy seriousness with which they oiled everything, and held up to them like a horrible mirror the foul fat face of Chadband. He saw that Mr. Podsnap thought too little of places outside England. But he saw that Mrs. Jellaby thought too much of them. In the last book he wrote he gives us, in Mr. Honeythunder, a hateful and wholesome picture of all the Liberal catchwords pouring out of one illiberal man. But perhaps the best evidence of this steadiness and sanity is the fact that, dogmatic as he was, he never tied himself to any passing dogma: he never got into any *cul de sac* of civic or economic fanaticism: he went down the broad road of the Revolution. He never admitted that, economically, we must make hells of workhouses, any more than Rousseau would have admitted it. He never said the State had no right to teach children or save their bones, any more than Danton would have said it. He was a fierce Radical; but he was never a Manchester Radical. He used the test of Utility, but he was never a Utilitarian. While economists were writing soft words he wrote "Hard Times," which Macaulay called "sullen Socialism," because it was not complacent Whiggism. But Dickens was never a Socialist any more than he was an Individualist; and, whatever else he was, he certainly was not sullen. He was not even a politician of any kind. He was simply a man of very clear, airy judgment on things that did not inflame his private temper, and he perceived that any theory that tried to run the living State entirely on one force and motive was probably nonsense. Whenever the Liberal philosophy had embedded in it something hard and heavy and lifeless, by an instinct he dropped it out. He was too romantic, perhaps, but he would have to do only with real things.

95

He may have cared too much about Liberty. But he cared nothing about "Laissez faire."

Now, among many interests of his contact with America this interest emerges as infinitely the largest and most striking, that it gave a final example of this queer, unexpected coolness and candour of his, this abrupt and sensational rationality. Apart altogether from any question of the accuracy of his picture of America, the American indignation was particularly natural and inevitable. For the large circumstances of the age must be taken into account. At the end of the previous epoch the whole of our Christian civilization had been startled from its sleep by trumpets to take sides in a bewildering Armageddon, often with eyes still misty. Germany and Austria found themselves on the side of the old order, France and America on the side of the new. England, as at the Reformation, took up eventually a dark middle position, maddeningly difficult to define. She created a democracy, but she kept an aristocracy: she reformed the House of Commons, but left the magistracy (as it is still) a mere league of gentlemen against the world. But underneath all this doubt and compromise there was in England a great and perhaps growing mass of dogmatic democracy; certainly thousands, probably millions expected a Republic in fifty years. And for these the first instinct was obvious. The first instinct was to look across the Atlantic to where lay a part of ourselves already Republican, the van of the advancing English on the road to liberty. Nearly all the great Liberals of the nineteenth century enormously idealized America. On the other hand to the Americans, fresh from their first epic of arms, the defeated mother country, with its coronets and county magistrates, was only a broken feudal keep.

So much is self-evident. But nearly halfway through

the nineteenth century there came out of England the
voice of a violent satirist. In its political quality it
seemed like the half-choked cry of the frustrated republic. It had no patience with the pretence that England
was already free, that we had gained all that was valuable from the Revolution. It poured a cataract of contempt on the so-called working compromises of England, on the oligarchic cabinets, on the two artificial
parties, on the government offices, on the J.P.'s, on the
vestries, on the voluntary charities. This satirist was
Dickens, and it must be remembered that he was not only
fierce, but uproariously readable. He really damaged
the things he struck at, a very rare thing. He stepped
up to the grave official of the vestry, really trusted by the
rulers, really feared like a god by the poor, and he tied
round his neck a name that choked him; never again
now can he be anything but Bumble. He confronted
the fine old English gentleman who gives his patriotic
services for nothing as a local magistrate, and he nailed
him up as Nupkins, an owl in open day. For to this
satire there is literally no answer; it cannot be denied
that a man like Nupkins can be and is a magistrate, so
long as we adopt the amazing method of letting the
rich man of a district actually be the judge in it. We can
only avoid the vision of the fact by shutting our eyes,
and imagining the nicest rich man we can think of; and
that, of course, is what we do. But Dickens, in this matter, was merely realistic; he merely asked us to look on
Nupkins, on the wild, strange thing that we had made.
Thus Dickens seemed to see England not at all as the
country where freedom slowly broadened down from
precedent to precedent, but as a rubbish heap of seventeenth century bad habits abandoned by everybody else.
That is, he looked at England almost with the eyes of
an American democrat.

And so, when the voice, swelling in volume, reached America and the Americans, the Americans said, "Here is a man who will hurry the old country along, and tip her kings and beadles into the sea. Let him come here, and we will show him a race of free men such as he dreams of, alive upon the ancient earth. Let him come here and tell the English of the divine democracy towards which he drives them. There he has a monarchy and an oligarchy to make game of. Here is a republic for him to praise." It seemed, indeed, a very natural sequel, that having denounced undemocratic England as the wilderness he should announce democratic America as the promised land. Any ordinary person would have prophesied that as he had pushed his rage at the old order almost to the edge of rant, he would push his encomium of the new order almost to the edge of cant. Amid a roar of republican idealism, compliments, hope, and anticipatory gratitude, the great democrat entered the great democracy. He looked about him; he saw a complete America, unquestionably progressive, unquestionably self-governing. Then, with a more than American coolness, and a more than American impudence, he sat down and wrote "Martin Chuzzlewit." That tricky and perverse sanity of his had mutinied again. Common sense is a wild thing, savage, and beyond rules; and it had turned on them and rent them.

The main course of action was as follows; and it is right to record it before we speak of the justice of it. When I speak of his sitting down and writing "Martin Chuzzlewit," I use, of course, an elliptical expression. He wrote the notes of the American part of "Martin Chuzzlewit" while he was still in America; but it was a later decision presumably that such impressions should go into a book, and it was little better than an after-thought that they should go into "Martin Chuzzlewit."

Dickens had an uncommonly bad habit (artistically speaking) of altering a story in the middle as he did in the case of "Our Mutual Friend." And it is on record that he only sent young Martin to America because he did not know what else to do with him, and because (to say truth) the sales were falling off. But the first action, which Americans regarded as an equally hostile one, was the publication of "American Notes," the history of which should first be given. His notion of visiting America had come to him as a very vague notion, even before the appearance of "The Old Curiosity Shop." But it had grown in him through the whole ensuing period in the plaguing and persistent way that ideas did grow in him and live with him. He contended against the idea in a certain manner. He had much to induce him to contend against it. Dickens was by this time not only a husband, but a father, the father of several children, and their existence made a difficulty in itself. His wife, he said, cried whenever the project was mentioned. But it was a point in him that he could never, with any satisfaction, part with a project. He had that restless optimism, that kind of nervous optimism, which would always tend to say "Yes"; which is stricken with an immortal repentance, if ever it says "No." The idea of seeing America might be doubtful, but the idea of not seeing America was dreadful. "To miss this opportunity would be a sad thing," he says. ". . . God willing, I think it *must* be managed somehow!" It was managed somehow. First of all he wanted to take his children as well as his wife. Final obstacles to this fell upon him, but they did not frustrate him. A serious illness fell on him; but that did not frustrate him. He sailed for America in 1842.

He landed in America, and he liked it. As John Forster very truly says, it is due to him, as well as to the great country that welcomed him, that his first good impression should be recorded, and that it should be "considered independently of any modification it afterwards underwent." But the modification it afterwards underwent was, as I have said above, simply a sudden kicking against cant, that is, against repetition. He was quite ready to believe that all Americans were free men. He would have believed it if they had not all told him so. He was quite prepared to be pleased with America. He would have been pleased with it if it had not been so much pleased with itself. The "modification" his view underwent did not arise from any "modification" of America as he first saw it. His admiration did not change because America changed. It changed because America did not change. The Yankees enraged him at last, not by saying different things, but by saying the same things. They were a republic; they were a new and vigorous nation; it seemed natural that they should say so to a famous foreigner first stepping on to their shore. But it seemed maddening that they should say so to each other in every car and drinking saloon from morning till night. It was not that the Americans in any way ceased from praising him. It was rather that they went on praising him. It was not merely that their praises of him sounded beautiful when he first heard them. Their praises of themselves sounded beautiful when he first heard them. That democracy was grand, and that Charles Dickens was a remarkable person, were two truths that he certainly never doubted to his dying day. But, as I say, it was a soulless repetition that stung his sense of humour out of sleep; it woke like a wild beast for hunting, the lion of his laughter. He had heard the truth once too often. He had heard the truth for the nine hundred and ninety-ninth time, and he suddenly saw that it was falsehood.

It is true that a particular circumstance sharpened and defined his disappointment. He felt very hotly, as he felt everything, whether selfish or unselfish, the injustice of the American piracies of English literature, resulting from the American copyright laws. He did not go to America with any idea of discussing this; when, some time afterwards, somebody said that he did, he violently rejected the view as only describable "in one of the shortest words in the English language." But his entry into America was almost triumphal; the rostrum or pulpit was ready for him; he felt strong enough to say anything. He had been most warmly entertained by many American men of letters, especially by Washington Irving, and in his consequent glow of confidence he stepped up to the dangerous question of American copyright. He made many speeches attacking the American law and theory of the matter as unjust to English writers and to American readers. The effect appears to have astounded him. "I believe there is no country," he writes, "on the face of the earth where there is less freedom of opinion on any subject in reference to which there is a broad difference of opinion than in this. There! I write the words with reluctance, disappointment, and sorrow; but I believe it from the bottom of my soul. . . . The notion that I, a man alone by myself in America, should venture to suggest to the Americans that there was one point on which they were neither just to their own countrymen nor to us, actually struck the boldest dumb! Washington Irving, Prescott, Hoffman, Bryant, Halleck, Dana, Washington Allston—every man who writes in this country is devoted to the question, and not one of them *dares* to raise his voice and complain of the atrocious state of the law. . . . The wonder is that a breathing man can be found with temerity enough to suggest to the Americans the possibility of their having done wrong. I wish you could have seen the faces that I saw down both sides of the table at Hartford when I began to talk about Scott. I wish you could have heard how I gave it out. My blood so boiled when I thought of the monstrous injustice that I felt as if I were twelve feet high when I thrust it down their throats."

That is almost a portrait of Dickens. We can almost see the erect little figure, its face and hair like a flame.

For such reasons, among others, Dickens was angry with America. But if America was angry with Dickens, there were also reasons for it. I do not think that the rage against his copyright speeches was, as he supposed, merely national insolence and self-satisfaction. America is a mystery to any good Englishman; but I think Dickens managed somehow to touch it on a queer nerve. There is one thing, at any rate, that must strike all Englishmen who have the good fortune to have American friends; that is, that while there is no materialism so crude or so material as American materialism, there is also no idealism so crude or so ideal as American idealism. America will always affect an Englishman as being soft in the wrong place and hard in the wrong place; coarse exactly where all civilized men are delicate, delicate exactly where all grown-up men are coarse. Some beautiful ideal runs through this people, but it runs aslant. The only existing picture in which the thing I mean has been embodied is in Stevenson's "Wrecker," in the blundering delicacy of Jim Pinkerton. America has a new delicacy, a coarse, rank refinement. But there is another way of embodying the idea, and that is to say this—that nothing is more likely than that the Americans thought it very shocking in Dickens, the divine author, to talk about being done out of money. Nothing would be more American than to expect a genius to be too high-toned for trade. It is certain that they deplored his selfishness in the matter, it is probable that they deplored his indelicacy. A beautiful young dreamer, with flowing brown hair, ought not to be even conscious of his copyrights. For it is quite unjust to say that the Americans worship the dollar. They really do worship intellect—another of the passing superstitions of our time.

If America had then this Pinkertonian propriety, this new, raw sensibility, Dickens was the man to rasp it. He was its precise opposite in every way. The decencies he did respect were old-fashioned and fundamental. On top of these he had that lounging liberty and comfort which can only be had on the basis of very old conventions, like the carelessness of gentlemen and the deliberation of rustics. He had no fancy for being strung up to that taut and quivering ideality demanded by American patriots and public speakers. And there was something else also, connected especially with the question of copyright and his own pecuniary claims. Dickens was not in the least desirous of being thought too "high-souled" to want his wages, nor was he in the least ashamed of asking for them. Deep in him (whether the modern reader likes the quality or no) was a sense very strong in the old Radicals—very strong especially in the old English Radicals—a sense of personal *rights,* one's own rights included, as something not merely useful but sacred. He did not think a claim any less just and solemn because it happened to be selfish; he did not divide claims into selfish and unselfish, but into right and wrong. It is significant that when he asked for his money, he never asked for it with that shamefaced cynicism, that sort of embarrassed brutality, with which the modern man of the world mutters something about business being business or looking after number one.

He asked for his money in a valiant and ringing voice, like a man asking for his honour. While his American critics were moaning and sneering at his interested motives as a disqualification, he brandished his interested motives like a banner. "It is nothing to them," he cries in astonishment, "that, of all men living, I am the greatest loser by it" (the Copyright Law). "It is nothing that I have a claim to speak and be heard." The thing they set up as a barrier he actually presents as a passport. They think that he, of all men, ought not to speak because he is interested. He thinks that he, of all men, ought to speak because he is wronged.

But this particular disappointment with America in the matter of the tyranny of its public opinion was not merely the expression of the fact that Dickens was a typical Englishman; that is, a man with a very sharp insistence upon individual freedom. It also worked back ultimately to that larger and vaguer disgust of which I have spoken—the disgust at the perpetual posturing of the people before a mirror. The tyranny was irritating, not so much because of the suffering it inflicted on the minority, but because of the awful glimpses that it gave of the huge and imbecile happiness of the majority. The very vastness of the vain race enraged him, its immensity, its unity, its peace. He was annoyed more with its contentment than with any of its discontents. The thought of that unthinkable mass of millions, every one of them saying that Washington was the greatest man on earth, and that the Queen lived in the Tower of London, rode his riotous fancy like a nightmare. But to the end he retained the outlines of his original republican ideal and lamented over America not as being too Liberal, but as not being Liberal enough. Among others, he used these somewhat remarkable words: "I tremble for a Radical coming here, unless he is a Radical on principle, by reason and reflection, and from the sense of right. I fear that if he were anything else he would return home a Tory. . . . I say no more on that head for two months from this time, save that I do fear that the heaviest blow ever dealt at liberty will be dealt by this country, in the failure of its example on the earth."

We are still waiting to see if that prediction has been fulfilled; but nobody can say that it has been falsified.

He went west on the great canals; he went south and touched the region of slavery; he saw America superficially indeed, but as a whole. And the great mass of his experience was certainly pleasant, though he vibrated with anticipatory passion against slave-holders, though he swore he would accept no public tribute in the slave country (a resolve which he broke under the pressure of the politeness of the South), yet his actual collisions with slavery and its upholders were few and brief. In these he bore himself with his accustomed vivacity and fire, but it would be a great mistake to convey the impression that his mental reaction against America was chiefly, or even largely, due to his horror at the Negro problem. Over and above the cant of which we have spoken, the weary rush of words, the chief complaint he made was a complaint against bad manners; and on a large view his anti-Americanism would seem to be more founded on spitting than on slavery. When, however, it did happen that the primary morality of man-owning came up for discussion, Dickens displayed an honourable impatience. One man, full of anti-abolitionist ardour, buttonholed him and bombarded him with the well-known argument in defence of slavery, that it was not to the financial interest of a slave-owner to damage or weaken his own slaves. Dickens, in telling the story of this interview, writes as follows: "I told him quietly that it was not a man's interest to get drunk, or to steal, or to game, or to indulge in any other vice; but he *did* indulge in it for all that. That cruelty and the abuse of irresponsible power were two of the bad passions of human nature, with the gratification of which considerations of interest or of ruin had nothing whatever to do. . . ." It is hardly possible to doubt that Dickens, in telling the man this, told him something sane and logical and unanswerable. But it is perhaps permissible to doubt whether he told it to him quietly.

He returned home in the spring of 1842, and in the later part of the year his "American Notes" appeared, and the cry against him that had begun over copyright swelled into a roar in his rear. Yet when we read the "Notes" we can find little offence in them, and, to say truth, less interest than usual. They are no true picture of America, or even of his vision of America, and this for two reasons. First, that he deliberately excluded from them all mention of that copyright question which had really given him his glimpse of how tyrannical a democracy can be. Second, that here he chiefly criticizes America for faults which are not, after all, especially American. For example, he is indignant with the inadequate character of the prisons, and compares them unfavourably with those in England, controlled by Lieutenant Tracey, and by Chesterton at Coldbath Fields, two reformers of prison discipline for whom he had a high regard. But it was a mere accident that American gaols were inferior to English. There was and is nothing in the American spirit to prevent their effecting all the reforms of Tracey and Chesterton, nothing to prevent their doing anything that money and energy and organization can do. America might have (for all I know, does have) a prison system cleaner and more humane and more efficient than any other in the world. And the evil genius of America might still remain—everything

might remain that makes Pogram or Chollop irritating
or absurd. And against the evil genius of America
Dickens was now to strike a second and a very different
blow.

In January, 1843, appeared the first number of the
novel called "Martin Chuzzlewit." The earlier part of
the book and the end, which have no connection with
America or the American problem, in any case require
a passing word. But except for the two gigantic grotesques on each side of the gateway of the tale, Pecksniff
and Mrs. Gamp, "Martin Chuzzlewit" will be chiefly
admired for its American excursion. It is a good satire
embedded in an indifferent novel. Mrs. Gamp is, indeed, a sumptuous study, laid on in those rich, oily,
almost greasy colours that go to make the English comic
characters, that make the very diction of Falstaff fat, and
quaking with jolly degradation. Pecksniff also is almost
perfect, and much too good to be true. The only other
thing to be noticed about him is that here, as almost
everywhere else in the novels, the best figures are at
their best when they have least to do. Dickens's characters are perfect as long as he can keep them out of
his stories. Bumble is divine until a dark and practical
secret is entrusted to him—as if anybody but a lunatic
would entrust a secret to Bumble. Micawber is noble
when he is doing nothing; but he is quite unconvincing
when he is spying on Uriah Heep, for obviously neither
Micawber nor any one else would employ Micawber as
a private detective. Similarly, while Pecksniff is the best
thing in the story, the story is the worst thing in Pecksniff. His plot against old Martin can only be described
by saying that it is as silly as old Martin's plot against
him. His fall at the end is one of the rare falls of
Dickens. Surely it was not necessary to take Pecksniff so
seriously. Pecksniff is a merely laughable character; he

is so laughable that he is lovable. Why take such trouble to unmask a man whose mask you have made transparent? Why collect all the characters to witness the exposure of a man in whom none of the characters believe? Why toil and triumph to have the laugh of a man who was only made to be laughed at?

But it is the American part of "Martin Chuzzlewit" which is our concern, and which is memorable. It has the air of a great satire; but if it is only a great slander, it is still great. His serious book on America was merely a squib, perhaps a damp squib. In any case, we all know that America will survive such serious books. But his fantastic book may survive America. It may survive America as "The Knights" has survived Athens. "Martin Chuzzlewit" has this quality of great satire that the critic forgets to ask whether the portrait is true to the original, because the portrait is so much more important than the original. Who cares whether Aristophanes correctly describes Kleon, who is dead, when he so perfectly describes the demagogue, who cannot die? Just as little, it may be, will some future age care whether the ancient civilization of the West, the lost cities of New York and St. Louis, were fairly depicted in the colossal monument of Elijah Pogram. For there is much more in the American episodes than their intoxicating absurdity; there is more than humour in the young man who made the speech about the British Lion, and said, "I taunt that lion. Alone I dare him"; or in the other man who told Martin that when he said that Queen Victoria did not live in the Tower of London he "fell into an error not uncommon among his countrymen." He has his finger on the nerve of an evil which was not only in his enemies, but in himself. The great democrat has hold of one of the dangers of democracy. The great optimist confronts a horrible nightmare of opti-

mism. Above all, the genuine Englishman attacks a sin
that is not merely American, but English also. The eternal, complacent iteration of patriotic half-truths; the
perpetual buttering of one's self all over with the
same stale butter; above all, the big defiances of small
enemies, or the very urgent challenges to very distant
enemies; the cowardice so habitual and unconscious that
it wears the plumes of courage—all this is an English
temptation as well as an American one. "Martin Chuzzlewit" may be a caricature of America. America may
be a caricature of England. But in the gravest college,
in the quietest country house of England, there is the
seed of the same essential madness that fills Dickens's
book, like an asylum, with brawling Chollops and raving Jefferson Bricks. That essential madness is the idea
that the good patriot is the man who feels at ease
about his country. This notion of patriotism was unknown in the little pagan republics where our European
patriotism began. It was unknown in the Middle Ages.
In the eighteenth century, in the making of modern
politics, a "patriot" meant a discontented man. It was
opposed to the word "courtier," which meant an up-
holder of the *status quo*. In all other modern countries,
especially in countries like France and Ireland, where
real difficulties have been faced, the word "patriot"
means something like a political pessimist. This view
and these countries have exaggerations and dangers of
their own; but the exaggeration and danger of England
is the same as the exaggeration and danger of *The
Watertoast Gazette*. The thing which is rather foolishly
called the Anglo-Saxon civilization is at present soaked
through with a weak pride. It uses great masses of men
not to procure discussion but to procure the pleasure of
unanimity; it uses masses like bolsters. It uses its organs
of public opinion not to warn the public, but to soothe

it. It really succeeds not only in ignoring the rest of the world, but actually in forgetting it. And when a civilization really forgets the rest of the world—lets it fall as something obviously dim and barbaric—then there is only one adjective for the ultimate fate of that civilization, and that adjective is "Chinese."

Martin Chuzzlewit's America is a mad-house: but it is a mad-house we are all on the road to. For completeness and even comfort are almost the definitions of insanity. The lunatic is the man who lives in a small world but thinks it is a large one: he is the man who lives in a tenth of the truth, and thinks it is the whole. The madman cannot conceive any cosmos outside a certain tale or conspiracy or vision. Hence the more clearly we see the world divided into Saxons and non-Saxons, into our splendid selves and the rest, the more certain we may be that we are slowly and quietly going mad. The more plain and satisfying our state appears, the more we may know that we are living in an unreal world. For the real world is not satisfying. The more clear become the colours and facts of Anglo-Saxon superiority, the more surely we may know we are in a dream. For the real world is not clear or plain. The real world is full of bracing bewilderments and brutal surprises. Comfort is the blessing and the curse of the English, and of Americans of the Pogram type also. With them it is a loud comfort, a wild comfort, a screaming and capering comfort; but comfort at bottom still. For there is but an inch of difference between the cushioned chamber and the padded cell.

CHAPTER VII

Dickens and Christmas

I N the July of 1844 Dickens went on an Italian tour, which he afterwards summarized in the book called "Pictures from Italy." They are, of course, very vivacious, but there is no great need to insist on them, considered as Italian sketches; there is no need whatever to worry about them as a phase of the mind of Dickens when he travelled out of England. He never travelled out of England. There is no trace in all these amusing pages that he really felt the great foreign things which lie in wait for us in the south of Europe, the Latin civilization, the Catholic Church, the art of the centre, the endless end of Rome. His travels are not travels in Italy, but travels in Dickensland. He sees amusing things; he describes them amusingly. But he would have seen things just as good in a street in Pimlico, and described them just as well. Few things were racier even in his raciest novel, than his description of the marionette play of the death of Napoleon. Nothing could be more perfect than the figure of the doctor, which had something wrong with its wires, and hence "hovered about the couch and delivered medical opinions in the air." Nothing could be better as a catching of the spirit of all popular drama than the colossal depravity of the wooden image of "Sir Udson Low." But there is nothing Italian about it. Dickens would have made just as good fun, indeed just the same fun, of a Punch and Judy show performing in Long Acre or Lincoln's Inn Fields.

Dickens uttered just and sincere satire on Plornish and Podsnap; but Dickens was as English as any Podsnap or any Plornish. He had a hearty humanitarianism, and a hearty sense of justice to all nations, so far as he understood it. But that very kind of humanitarianism, that very kind of justice, were English. He was the Englishman of the type that made Free Trade, the most English of all things, since it was at once calculating and optimistic. He respected catacombs and gondolas, but that very respect was English. He wondered at brigands and volcanoes, but that very wonder was English. The very conception that Italy consists of these things was an English conception. The root things he never understood, the Roman legend, the ancient life of the Mediterranean, the world-old civilization of the vine and olive, the mystery of the immutable Church. He never understood these things, and I am glad he never understood them: he could only have understood them by ceasing to be the inspired cockney that he was, the rousing English Radical of the great Radical age in England. That spirit of his was one of the things that we have had which were truly national. All other forces we have borrowed, especially those which flatter us most. Imperialism is foreign, socialism is foreign, militarism is foreign, education is foreign, strictly even Liberalism is foreign. But Radicalism was our own; as English as the hedgerows.

Dickens abroad, then, was for all serious purposes simply the Englishman abroad; the Englishman abroad is for all serious purposes, simply the Englishman at home. Of this generalization one modification must be made. Dickens did feel a direct pleasure in the bright and busy exterior of the French life, the clean caps, the coloured uniforms, the skies like blue enamel, the little green trees, the little white houses, the scene picked out in primary colours, like a child's picture-book. This he felt, and this he put (by a stroke of genius) into the mouth of Mrs. Lirriper, a London landlady on a holiday: for Dickens always knew that it is the simple and not the subtle who feel differences; and he saw all his colours through the clear eyes of the poor. And in thus taking to his heart the streets as it were, rather than the spires of the Continent, he showed beyond question that combination of which we have spoken—of common sense with uncommon sensibility. For it is for the sake of the streets and shops and the coats and hats, that we should go abroad; they are far better worth going to see than the castles and cathedrals and Roman camps. For the wonders of the world are the same all over the world, at least all over the European world. Castles that throw valleys in shadow, minsters that strike the sky, roads so old that they seem to have been made by the gods, these are in all Christian countries. The marvels of man are at all our doors. A labourer hoeing turnips in Sussex has no need to be ignorant that the bones of Europe are the Roman roads. A clerk living in Lambeth has no need not to know that there was a Christian art exuberant in the thirteenth century; for only across the river he can see the live stones of the Middle Ages surging together towards the stars. But exactly the things that do strike the traveller as extraordinary are the ordinary things, the food, the clothes, the vehicles; the strange things are cosmopolitan, the common things are national and peculiar. Cologne spire is lifted on the same arches as Canterbury; but the thing you cannot see out of Germany is a German beer-garden. There is no need for a Frenchman to go to look at Westminster Abbey as a piece of English architecture; it is not, in the special sense, a piece of English architecture. But a hansom cab is a piece of English architecture; a thing produced by the peculiar poetry of our cities, a symbol of a certain reckless comfort which is really English; a thing to draw a pilgrimage of the nations. The imaginative Englishman will be found all day in a *café;* the imaginative Frenchman in a hansom cab.

This sort of pleasure Dickens took in the Latin life; but no deeper kind. And the strongest of all possible indications of his fundamental detachment from it can be found in one fact. A great part of the time that he was in Italy he was engaged in writing "The Chimes," and such Christmas tales, tales of Christmas in the English towns, tales full of fog and snow and hail and happiness.

Dickens could find in any street divergences between man and man deeper than the divisions of nations. His fault was to exaggerate differences. He could find types almost as distinct as separate tribes of animals in his own brain and his own city, those two homes of a magnificent chaos. The only two southerners introduced prominently into his novels, the two in "Little Dorrit," are popular English foreigners, I had almost said stage foreigners. Villainy is, in English eyes, a southern trait, therefore one of the foreigners is villainous. Vivacity is, in English eyes, another southern trait, therefore the other foreigner is vivacious. But we can see from the outlines of both that Dickens did not have to go to Italy to get them. While poor panting millionaires, poor tired earls and poor God-forsaken American men of culture are plodding about Italy for literary inspiration, Charles Dickens made up the whole of that Italian romance (as

I strongly suspect) from the faces of two London organ-grinders.

In the sunlight of the southern world, he was still dreaming of the firelight of the north. Among the palaces and the white campanile, he shut his eyes to see Marylebone and dreamed a lovely dream of chimney-pots. He was not happy he said, without streets. The very foulness and smoke of London were lovable in his eyes and fill his Christmas tales with a vivid vapour. In the clear skies of the south he saw afar off the fog of London like a sunset cloud and longed to be in the core of it.

This Christmas tone of Dickens, in connection with his travels, is a matter that can only be expressed by a parallel with one of his other works. Much the same that has here been said of his "Pictures from Italy" may be said about his "Child's History of England"; with the difference that while the "Pictures from Italy" does in a sense add to his fame, the "History of England" in almost every sense detracts from it. But the nature of the limitation is the same. What Dickens was travelling in distant lands, that he was travelling in distant ages; a sturdy, sentimental English Radical with a large heart and a narrow mind. He could not help falling into that besetting sin or weakness of the modern progressive, the habit of regarding the contemporary questions as the eternal questions and the latest word as the last. He could not get out of his head the instinctive conception that the real problem before St. Dunstan was whether he should support Lord John Russell or Sir Robert Peel. He could not help seeing the remotest peaks lit up by the raging bonfire of his own passionate political crisis. He lived for the instant and its urgency; that is, he did what St. Dunstan did. He lived in an eternal present like all simple men. It is indeed "A Child's History of

England"; but the child is the writer and not the reader.

But Dickens in his cheapest cockney utilitarianism, was not only English, but unconsciously historic. Upon him descended the real tradition of "Merry England," and not upon the pallid mediævalists who thought they were reviving it. The Pre-Raphaelites, the Gothicists, the admirers of the Middle Ages, had in their subtlety and sadness the spirit of the present day. Dickens had in his buffoonery and bravery the spirit of the Middle Ages. He was much more mediæval in his attacks on mediævalism than they were in their defences of it. It was he who had the things of Chaucer, the love of large jokes and long stories and brown ale and all the white roads of England. Like Chaucer he loved story within story, every man telling a tale. Like Chaucer he saw something openly comic in men's motley trades. Sam Weller would have been a great gain to the Canterbury Pilgrimage and told an admirable story. Rossetti's Damozel would have been a great bore, regarded as too fast by the Prioress and too priggish by the Wife of Bath. It is said that in the somewhat sickly Victorian revival of feudalism which was called "Young England," a nobleman hired a hermit to live in his grounds. It is also said that the hermit struck for more beer. Whether this anecdote be true or not, it is always told as showing a collapse from the ideal of the Middle Ages to the level of the present day. But in the mere act of striking for beer the holy man was very much more "mediæval" than the fool who employed him.

It would be hard to find a better example of this than Dickens's great defence of Christmas. In fighting for Christmas he was fighting for the old European festival, Pagan and Christian, for that trinity of eating, drinking and praying which to moderns appears irreverent, for the holy day which is really a holiday. He had himself

the most babyish ideas about the past. He supposed the
Middle Ages to have consisted of tournaments and tor-
ture-chambers, he supposed himself to be a brisk man
of the manufacturing age, almost a Utilitarian. But for
all that he defended the mediæval feast which was going
out against the Utilitarianism which was coming in. He
could only see all that was bad in mediævalism. But he
fought for all that was good in it. And he was all the
more really in sympathy with the old strength and simplicity because he only knew that it was good and did
not know that it was old. He cared as little for mediævalism as the mediævals did. He cared as much as they did
for lustiness and virile laughter and sad tales of good
lovers and pleasant tales of good livers. He would have
been very much bored by Ruskin and Walter Pater if
they had explained to him the strange sunset tints of
Lippi and Botticelli. He had no pleasure in looking on
the dying Middle Ages. But he looked on the living
Middle Ages, on a piece of the old uproarious supersti-
tion still unbroken; and he hailed it like a new religion.
The Dickens character ate pudding to an extent at
which the modern mediævalists turned pale. They
would do every kind of honour to an old observance,
except observing it. They would pay to a Church feast
every sort of compliment except feasting.

And (as I have said) as were his unconscious relations
to our European past, so were his unconscious relations
to England. He imagined himself to be, if anything, a
sort of cosmopolitan; at any rate to be a champion of
the charms and merits of continental lands against the
arrogance of our island. But he was in truth very much
more a champion of the old and genuine England against
that comparatively cosmopolitan England which we
have all lived to see. And here again the supreme example is Christmas. Christmas is, as I have said, one of

numberless old European feasts of which the essence is the combination of religion with merry-making. But among those feasts it is also especially and distinctively English in the style of its merry-making and even in the style of its religion. For the character of Christmas (as distinct, for instance, from the continental Easter) lies chiefly in two things: first on the terrestrial side the note of comfort rather than the note of brightness; and on the spiritual side, Christian charity rather than Christian ecstasy. And comfort is, like charity, a very English instinct. Nay, comfort is, like charity, an English merit; though our comfort may and does degenerate into materialism, just as our charity may (and does) degenerate into laxity and make-believe.

This ideal of comfort belongs peculiarly to England; it belongs peculiarly to Christmas; above all it belongs pre-eminently to Dickens. And it is astonishingly misunderstood. It is misunderstood by the continent of Europe, it is, if possible, still more misunderstood by the English of to-day. On the Continent the restaurateurs provide us with raw beef, as if we were savages; yet old English cooking takes as much care as French. And in England has arisen a parvenu patriotism which represents the English as everything but English; as a blend of Chinese stoicism, Latin militarism, Prussian rigidity, and American bad taste. And so England, whose fault is gentility and whose virtue is geniality, England with her tradition of the great gay gentlemen of Elizabeth, is represented to the four quarters of the world (as in Mr. Kipling's religious poems) in the enormous image of a solemn cad. And because it is very difficult to be comfortable in the suburbs, the suburbs have voted that comfort is a gross and material thing. Comfort, especially this vision of Christmas comfort, is the reverse of a gross or material thing. It is far more poetical, properly speaking, than the Garden of Epicurus. It is far more artistic than the Palace of Art. It is more artistic because it is based upon a contrast, a contrast between the fire and wine within the house and the winter and the roaring rains without. It is far more poetical, because there is in it a note of defence, almost of war; a note of being besieged by the snow and hail; of making merry in the belly of a fort. The man who said that an Englishman's house is his castle said much more than he meant. The Englishman thinks of his house as something fortified, and provisioned, and his very surliness is at root romantic. And this sense would naturally be strongest in wild winter nights, when the lowered portcullis and the lifted drawbridge do not merely bar people out, but bar people in. The Englishman's house is most sacred, not merely when the King cannot enter it, but when the Englishman cannot get out of it.

This comfort, then, is an abstract thing, a principle. The English poor shut all their doors and windows till their rooms reek like the Black Hole. They are suffering for an idea. Mere animal hedonism would not dream, as we English do, of winter feasts and little rooms, but of eating fruit in large and idle gardens. Mere sensuality would desire to please all its senses. But to our good dreams this dark and dangerous background is essential; the highest pleasure we can imagine is a defiant pleasure, a happiness that stands at bay. The word "comfort" is not indeed the right word, it conveys too much of the slander of mere sense; the true word is "cosiness," a word not translatable. One, at least, of the essentials of it is smallness, smallness in preference to largeness, smallness for smallness's sake. The merry-maker wants a pleasant parlour, he would not give twopence for a pleasant continent. In our difficult time, of course, a fight for mere space has become necessary. Instead of being greedy for ale and Christmas pudding we are greedy for mere air, an equally sensual appetite. In abnormal conditions this is wise; and the illimitable veldt is an excellent thing for nervous people. But our fathers were large and healthy enough to make a thing humane, and not worry about whether it was hygienic. They were big enough to get into small rooms.

Of this quite deliberate and artistic quality in the close Christmas chamber, the standing evidence is Dickens in Italy. He created these dim firelit tales like little dim red jewels, as an artistic necessity, in the centre of an endless summer. Amid the white cities of Tuscany he hungered for something romantic, and wrote about a rainy Christmas. Amid the pictures of the Uffizi he starved for something beautiful, and fed his memory on London fog. His feeling for the fog was especially poignant and typical. In the first of his Christmas tales, the popular "A Christmas Carol," he suggested the very soul of it in one simile, when he spoke of the dense air, suggesting that "Nature was brewing on a large scale." The sense of the thick atmosphere as something to eat or drink, something not only solid but satisfactory, may seem almost insane, but it is no exaggeration of Dickens's emotion. We speak of a fog "that you could cut with a knife." Dickens would have liked the phrase as suggesting that the fog was a colossal cake. He liked even more his own phrase of the Titanic brewery, and no dream would have given him a wilder pleasure than to grope his way to some such tremendous vats and drink the ale of the giants.

There is a current prejudice against fogs, and Dickens, perhaps, is their only poet. Considered hygienically no doubt this may be more or less excusable. But, considered poetically, fog is not undeserving, it has a real significance. We have in our great cities abolished the clean and sane darkness of the country. We have outlawed night and sent her wandering in wild meadows; we have lit eternal watch-fires against her return. We have made a new cosmos, and as a consequence our own sun and stars. And, as a consequence also, and most justly, we have made our own darkness. Just as every lamp is a warm human moon, so every fog is a rich human nightfall. If it were not for this mystic accident we should never see darkness, and he who has never seen darkness has never seen the sun. Fog for us is the chief form of that outward pressure which compresses mere luxury into real comfort. It makes the world small, in the same spirit as in that common and happy cry that the world is small, meaning that it is full of friends. The first man that emerges out of the mist with a light, is for us Prometheus, a saviour bringing fire to men. He is that greatest and best of all men, greater than the heroes, better than the saints, Man Friday. Every rumble of a cart, every cry in the distance, marks the heart of humanity beating undaunted in the darkness. It is wholly human; man toiling in his own cloud. If real darkness is like the embrace of God, this is the dark embrace of man.

In such a sacred cloud the tale called "A Christmas Carol" begins, the first and most typical of all his Christmas tales. It is not irrelevant to dilate upon the geniality of this darkness, because it is characteristic of Dickens that his atmospheres are more important than his stories. The Christmas atmosphere is more important than Scrooge, or the ghosts either; in a sense, the background is more important than the figures. The same thing may be noticed in his dealings with that other atmosphere (besides that of good humour) which he excelled in creating, an atmosphere of mystery and wrong, such as that which gathers round Mrs. Clennam, rigid in her chair, or old Miss Havisham, ironically robed as a bride. Here again the atmosphere altogether eclipses the story, which often seems disappointing in comparison. The secrecy is sensational; the secret is tame. The surface of the thing seems more awful than the core of it. It seems almost as if these grisly figures, Mrs. Chadband and Mrs. Clennam, Miss Havisham and Miss Flite, Nemo and Sally Brass, were keeping something back from the author as well as from the reader. When the book closes we do not know their real secret. They soothed the optimistic Dickens with something less terrible than the truth. The dark house of Arthur Clennam's childhood really depresses us; it is a true glimpse into that quiet street in hell, where live the children of that unique dispensation which theologians call Calvinism and Christians devil-worship. But some stranger crime had really been done there, some more monstrous blasphemy or human sacrifice than the suppression of some silly document advantageous to the silly Dorrits. Something worse than a common tale of jilting lay behind the masquerade and madness of the awful Miss Havisham. Something worse was whispered by the misshapen Quilp to the sinister Sally in that wild, wet summer-house by the river, something worse than the clumsy plot against the clumsy Kit. These dark pictures seem almost as if they were literally visions; things, that is, that Dickens saw but did not understand.

And as with his backgrounds of gloom, so with his backgrounds of good-will, in such tales as "A Christmas Carol." The tone of the tale is kept throughout in a happy monotony, though the tale is everywhere irregular and in some places weak. It has the same kind of artistic unity that belongs to a dream. A dream may begin with the end of the world and end with a tea-party; but either the end of the world will seem as trivial as a tea-party or that tea-party will be as terrible as the day of doom. The incidents change wildly; the story scarcely changes at all. "A Christmas Carol" is a kind of philanthropic dream, an enjoyable nightmare, in which the scenes shift bewilderingly and seem as miscellaneous as the pictures in a scrap-book, but in which there is one constant state of the soul, a state of rowdy benediction and a hunger for human faces. The beginning is about a winter day and a miser; yet the beginning is in no way bleak. The author starts with a kind of happy howl; he bangs on our door like a drunken carol singer; his style is festive and popular; he compares the snow and hail to philanthropists who "come down handsomely"; he compares the fog to unlimited beer. Scrooge is not really inhuman at the beginning any more than he is at the end. There is a heartiness in his inhospitable sentiments that is akin to humour and therefore to humanity; he is only a crusty old bachelor, and had (I strongly suspect) given away turkeys secretly all his life. The beauty and the real blessing of the story do not lie in the mechanical plot of it, the repentance of Scrooge, probable or improbable; they lie in the great furnace of real happiness that glows through Scrooge and everything round him; that great furnace, the heart of Dickens. Whether the Christmas visions would or would not convert Scrooge, they convert us. Whether or no the visions were evoked by real Spirits of the Past, Present, and Future, they were evoked by that truly exalted order of angels who are correctly called High Spirits. They are impelled and sustained by a quality which our contemporary artists ignore or almost deny, but which in a life decently lived is as normal and attainable as sleep, positive, passionate, conscious joy. The story sings from end to end like a happy man going home; and, like a happy and good man, when it cannot sing it yells. It is lyric and exclamatory, from the first exclamatory words of it. It is strictly a Christmas Carol.

Dickens, as has been said, went to Italy with this kindly cloud still about him, still meditating on Yule mysteries. Among the olives and the orange-trees he wrote his second great Christmas tale, "The Chimes" (at Genoa in 1844), a Christmas tale only differing from "A Christmas Carol" in being fuller of the grey rains of winter and the north. "The Chimes" is, like the "Carol," an appeal for charity and mirth, but it is a stern and fighting appeal: if the other is a Christmas carol, this is a Christmas war-song. In it Dickens hurled himself with even more than his usual militant joy and scorn into an attack upon a cant, which he said made his blood boil. This cant was nothing more nor less than the whole tone taken by three-quarters of the political and economic world towards the poor. It was a vague and vulgar Benthamism with a rollicking Tory touch in it. It explained to the poor their duties with a cold and coarse philanthropy unendurable by any free man. It had also at its command a kind of brutal banter, a loud good-humour which Dickens sketches savagely in Alderman Cute. He fell furiously on all their ideas: the cheap advice to live cheaply, the base advice to live basely, above all, the preposterous primary assumption that the rich are to advise the poor and not the poor the rich. There were and are hundreds of these benevolent bullies. Some say that the poor should give up having children, which means that they should give up their great virtue of sexual sanity. Some say that they should give up "treating" each other, which means that they should give up all that remains to them of the virtue of hospitality. Against all of this Dickens thundered very thor-

oughly in "The Chimes." It may be remarked in passing
that this affords another instance of a confusion already
referred to, the confusion whereby Dickens supposed
himself to be exalting the present over the past, whereas
he was really dealing deadly blows at things strictly peculiar to the present. Embedded in this very book is a
somewhat useless interview between Trotty Veck and
the church bells, in which the latter lectures the former
for having supposed (why I don't know) that they were
expressing regret for the disappearance of the Middle
Ages. There is no reason why Trotty Veck or any one
else should idealize the Middle Ages, but certainly he
was the last man in the world to be asked to idealize
the nineteenth century, seeing that the smug and stingy
philosophy, which poisons his life through the book,
was an exclusive creation of that century. But, as I have
said before, the fieriest mediævalist may forgive Dickens
for disliking the good things the Middle Ages took away,
considering how he loved whatever good things the
Middle Ages left behind. It matters very little that he
hated old feudal castles when they were already old. It
matters very much that he hated the New Poor Law
while it was still new.

The moral of this matter in "The Chimes" is essential. Dickens had sympathy with the poor in the Greek
and literal sense; he suffered with them mentally; for
the things that irritated them were the things that irritated him. He did not pity the people, or even champion
the people, or even merely love the people; in this matter he was the people. He alone in our literature is the
voice not merely of the social substratum, but even of
the subconsciousness of the substratum. He utters the
secret anger of the humble. He says what the uneducated only think, or even only feel, about the educated.
And in nothing is he so genuinely such a voice as in

this fact of his fiercest mood being reserved for methods that are counted scientific and progressive. Pure and exalted atheists talk themselves into believing that the working-classes are turning with indignant scorn from the churches. The working-classes are not indignant against the churches in the least. The things the working-classes really are indignant against are the hospitals. The people has no definite disbelief in the temples of theology. The people has a very fiery and practical disbelief in the temples of physical science. The things the poor hate are the modern things, the rationalistic things —doctors, inspectors, poor law guardians, professional philanthropy. They never showed any reluctance to be helped by the old and corrupt monasteries. They will often die rather than be helped by the modern and efficient workhouse. Of all this anger, good or bad, Dickens is the voice of an accusing energy. When, in "A Christmas Carol," Scrooge refers to the surplus population, the Spirit tells him, very justly, not to speak till he knows what the surplus is and where it is. The implication is severe but sound. When a group of superciliously benevolent economists look down into the abyss for the surplus population, assuredly there is only one answer that should be given to them; and that is to say, "If there is a surplus, you are a surplus." And if any one were ever cut off, they would be. If the barricades went up in our streets and the poor became masters, I think the priests would escape, I fear the gentlemen would; but I believe the gutters would be simply running with the blood of philanthropists.

Lastly, he was at one with the poor in this chief matter of Christmas, in the matter, that is, of special festivity. There is nothing on which the poor are more criticized than on the point of spending large sums on small feasts; and though there are material difficulties, there is nothing in which they are more right. It is said that a Boston paradox-monger said, "Give us the luxuries of life and we will dispense with the necessities." But it is the whole human race that says it, from the first savage wearing feathers instead of clothes to the last coster-monger having a treat instead of three meals.

The third of his Christmas stories, "The Cricket on the Hearth," calls for no extensive comment, though it is very characteristic. It has all the qualities which we have called dominant qualities in his Christmas senti-ment. It has cosiness, that is the comfort that depends upon a discomfort surrounding it. It has a sympathy with the poor, and especially with the extravagance of the poor; with what may be called the temporary wealth of the poor. It has the sentiment of the hearth, that is, the sentiment of the open fire being the red heart of the room. That open fire is the veritable flame of Eng-land, still kept burning in the midst of a mean civiliza-tion of stoves. But everything that is valuable in "The Cricket on the Hearth" is perhaps as well expressed in the title as it is in the story. The tale itself, in spite of some of those inimitable things that Dickens never failed to say, is a little too comfortable to be quite convincing. "A Christmas Carol" is the conversion of an anti-Christ-mas character. "The Chimes" is a slaughter of anti-Christmas characters. "The Cricket," perhaps, fails for lack of this crusading note. For everything has its weak side, and when full justice has been done to this neg-lected note of poetic comfort, we must remember that it has its very real weak side. The defect of it in the work of Dickens was that he tended sometimes to pile up the cushions until none of the characters could move. He is so much interested in effecting his state of static hap-piness that he forgets to make a story at all. His princes at the start of the story begin to live happily ever afterwards. We feel this strongly in "Master Humphrey's Clock," and we feel it sometimes in these Christmas stories. He makes his characters so comfortable that his characters begin to dream and drivel. And he makes his reader so comfortable that his reader goes to sleep.

The actual tale of the carrier and his wife sounds somewhat sleepily in our ears; we cannot keep our attention fixed on it, though we are conscious of a kind of warmth from it as from a great wood fire. We know so well that everything will soon be all right that we do not suspect when the carrier suspects, and are not frightened when the gruff Tackleton growls. The sound of the Christmas festivities at the end comes fainter on our ears than did the shout of the Cratchits or the bells of Trotty Veck. All the good figures that followed Scrooge when he came growling out of the fog fade into the fog again.

CHAPTER VIII

The Time of Transition

DICKENS was back in London by the June of 1845. About this time he became the first editor of *The Daily News,* a paper which he had largely planned and suggested, and which, I trust, remembers its semi-divine origin. That his thoughts had been running, as suggested in the last chapter, somewhat monotonously on his Christmas domesticities, is again suggested by the rather singular fact that he originally wished *The Daily News* to be called *The Cricket.* Probably he was haunted again with his old vision of a homely, tale-telling periodical such as had broken off in "Master Humphrey's Clock." About this time, however, he was peculiarly unsettled. Almost as soon as he had taken the editorship he threw it up; and having only recently come back to England, he soon made up his mind to go back to the Continent. In the May of 1846 he ran over to Switzerland and tried to write "Dombey and Son" at Lausanne. Tried to, I say, because his letters are full of an angry impotence. He could not get on. He attributed this especially to his love of London and his loss of it, "the absence of streets and numbers of figures. . . . *My* figures seem disposed to stagnate without crowds about them."

But he also, with shrewdness, attributed it more generally to the laxer and more wandering life he had led for the last two years, the American tour, the Italian tour, diversified, generally speaking, only with slight literary productions. His ways were never punctual or healthy, but they were also never unconscientious as far as work was concerned. If he walked all night he could write all day. But in this strange exile or interregnum he did not seem able to fall into any habits, even bad habits. A restlessness beyond all his experience had fallen for a season upon the most restless of the children of men.

It may be a mere coincidence: but this break in his life very nearly coincided with the important break in his art. "Dombey and Son," planned in all probability some time before, was destined to be the last of a quite definite series, the early novels of Dickens. The difference between the books from the beginning up to "Dombey," and the books from "David Copperfield" to the end may be hard to state dogmatically, but is evident to every one with any literary sense. Very coarsely, the case may be put by saying that he diminished, in the story as a whole, the practice of pure caricature. Still more coarsely it may be put in the phrase that he began to practise realism. If we take Mr. Stiggins, say, as a clergyman depicted at the beginning of his literary career, and Mr. Crisparkle, say, as a clergyman depicted at the end of it, it is evident that the difference does not merely consist in the fact that the first is a less desirable clergyman than the second. It consists in the nature of our desire for either of them. The glory of Mr. Crisparkle partly consists in the fact that he might really exist anywhere, in any country town into which we may happen to stray. The glory of Mr. Stiggins wholly consists in the fact that he could not possibly exist anywhere except in the head of Dickens. Dickens has the secret recipe of that divine dish. In some sense, therefore, when we say that he became less of a caricaturist we mean that he became less of a creator. That original violent vision of all things which he had seen from his boyhood began to be mixed with other men's milder visions and with the light of common day. He began to understand and practise other than his own mad merits; began to have some movement towards the merits of other writers, towards the mixed emotion of Thackeray, or the solidity of George Eliot. And this must be said for the process; that the fierce wine of Dickens could endure some dilution. On the whole, perhaps, his primal personalism was all the better when surging against some saner restraints. Perhaps a flavour of strong Stiggins goes a long way. Perhaps the colossal Crummles might be cut down into six or seven quite credible characters. For my own part, for reasons which I shall afterwards mention, I am in real doubt about the advantage of this realistic education of Dickens. I am not sure that it made his books better; but I am sure it made them less bad. He made fewer mistakes undoubtedly; he succeeded in eliminating much of the mere rant or cant of his first books; he threw away much of the old padding, all the more annoying, perhaps, in a literary sense, because he did not mean it for padding, but for essential eloquence. But he did not produce anything actually better than Mr. Chuckster. But then there is nothing better than Mr. Chuckster. Certain works of art, such as the Venus of Milo, exhaust our aspiration. Upon the whole this may, perhaps, be safely said of the transition. Those who have any doubt about Dickens can have no doubt of the superiority of the later books. Beyond question they have less of what annoys us in Dickens. But do not, if you are in the company of any ardent adorers of Dickens (as I hope for your sake you are), do not insist too urgently and exclusively on the splendour of Dickens's last works, or they will discover that you do not like him.

"Dombey and Son" is the last novel in the first manner: "David Copperfield" is the first novel in the last. The increase in care and realism in the second of the two is almost startling. Yet even in "Dombey and Son" we can see the coming of a change, however faint, if we compare it with his first fantasies, such as "Nicholas Nickleby" or "The Old Curiosity Shop." The central story is still melodrama, but it is much more tactful and effective melodrama. Melodrama is a form of art, legitimate like any other, as noble as farce, almost as noble as pantomime. The essence of melodrama is that it appeals to the moral sense in a highly simplified state, just as farce appeals to the sense of humour in a highly simplified state. Farce creates people who are so intellectually simple as to hide in packing-cases or pretend to be their own aunts. Melodrama creates people so morally simple as to kill their enemies in Oxford Street, and repent on seeing their mother's photograph. The object of the simplification in farce and melodrama is the same, and quite artistically legitimate, the object of gaining a resounding rapidity of action which subtleties would obstruct. And this can be done well or ill. The simplified villain can be a spirited charcoal sketch or a mere black smudge. Carker is a spirited charcoal sketch: Ralph Nickleby is a mere black smudge. The tragedy of Edith Dombey teems with unlikelihood, but it teems with life. That Dombey should give his own wife censure through his own business manager is impossible, I will not say in a gentleman, but in a person of ordinary sane self-conceit. But once having got the inconceivable trio before the footlights, Dickens gives us good ringing dialogue, very different from the mere rants in which Ralph Nickleby figures in the unimaginable character of a rhetorical money-lender. And there is another point of technical improvement in this book over such books as "Nicholas Nickleby." It has not only a basic idea, but a good basic idea. There is a real artistic opportunity in the conception of a solemn and selfish man of affairs, feeling for his male heir his first and last emotion, mingled of a thin flame of tenderness and a strong flame of pride. But with all these possibilities, the serious episode of the Dombeys serves ultimately only to show how unfitted Dickens was for such things, how fitted he was for something opposite.

The incurable poetic character, the hopelessly non-realistic character of Dickens's essential genius could not have a better example than the story of the Dombeys. For the story itself is probable; it is the treatment that makes it unreal. In attempting to paint the dark pagan devotion of the father (as distinct from the ecstatic and Christian devotion of the mother), Dickens was painting something that was really there. This is no wild theme, like the wanderings of Nell's grandfather, or the marriage of Gride. A man of Dombey's type would love his son as he loves Paul. He would neglect his daughter as he neglects Florence. And yet we feel the utter unreality of it all, while we feel the utter reality of monsters like Stiggins or Mantalini. Dickens could only work in his own way, and that way was the wild way. We may almost say this: that he could only make his characters probable if he was allowed to make them impossible. Give him license to say and do anything, and he could create beings as vivid as our own aunts and uncles. Keep him to likelihood and he could not tell the plainest tale so as to make it seem likely. The story of "Pickwick" is credible, although it is not possible. The story of Florence Dombey is incredible although it is true.

An excellent example can be found in the same story. Major Bagstock is a grotesque, and yet he contains touch after touch of Dickens's quiet and sane observation of things as they are. He was always most accurate when he was most fantastic. Dombey and Florence are perfectly reasonable, but we simply know that they do not exist. The Major is mountainously exaggerated, but we all feel that we have met him at Brighton. Nor is the rationale of the paradox difficult to see; Dickens exaggerated when he had found a real truth to exaggerate. It is a deadly error (an error at the back of much of the false placidity of our politics) to suppose that lies are told with excess and luxuriance, and truths told with modesty and restraint. Some of the most frantic lies on the face of life are told with modesty and restraint; for the simple reason that only modesty and restraint will save them. Many official declarations are just as dignified as Mr. Dombey, because they are just as fictitious. On the other hand, the man who has found a truth dances about like a boy who has found a shilling; he breaks into extravagances, as the Christian churches broke into gargoyles. In one sense truth alone can be exaggerated; nothing else can stand the strain. The outrageous Bagstock is a glowing and glaring exaggeration of a thing we have all seen in life—the worst and most dangerous of all its hypocrisies. For the worst and most dangerous hypocrite is not he who affects unpopular virtue, but he who affects popular vice. The jolly fellow of the saloon bar and the racecourse is the real deceiver of mankind; he has misled more than any false prophet, and his victims cry to him out of hell. The excellence of the Bagstock conception can best be seen if we compare it with the much weaker and more improbable knavery of Pecksniff. It would not be worth a man's while, with any worldly object, to pretend to be a holy and high-minded architect. The world does not admire holy and high-minded architects. The world does admire rough and tough old army men who swear at waiters and wink at women. Major Bagstock is simply the perfect prophecy of that decadent jingoism which corrupted England of late years. England has been duped, not by the cant of goodness, but by the cant of badness. It has been fascinated by a quite fictitious cynicism, and reached that last and strangest of all impostures in which the mask is as repulsive as the face.

"Dombey and Son" provides us with yet another instance of this general fact in Dickens. He could only get to the most solemn emotions adequately if he got to them through the grotesque. He could only, so to speak, really get into the inner chamber by coming down the chimney, like his own most lovable lunatic in "Nicholas Nickleby." A good example is such a character as Toots. Toots is what none of Dickens's dignified characters are, in the most serious sense, a true lover. He is the twin of Romeo. He has passion, humility, self-knowledge, a mind lifted into all magnanimous thoughts, everything that goes with the best kind of romantic love. His excellence in the art of love can only be expressed by the somewhat violent expression that he is as good a lover as Walter Gay is a bad one. Florence surely deserved her father's scorn if she could prefer Gay to Toots. It is neither a joke nor any kind of exaggeration to say that in the vacillations of Toots, Dickens not only came nearer to the psychology of true love than he ever came elsewhere, but nearer than any one else ever came. To ask for the loved one, and then not to dare to cross the threshold, to be invited by her, to long to accept, and

then to lie in order to decline, these are the funny
things that Mr. Toots did, and that every honest man
who yells with laughter at him has done also. For the
moment, however, I only mention this matter as a
pendent case to the case of Major Bagstock, an example
of the way in which Dickens had to be ridiculous in
order to begin to be true. His characters that begin
solemn end futile; his characters that begin frivolous
end solemn in the best sense. His foolish figures are
not only more entertaining than his serious figures, they
are also much more serious. The Marchioness is not
only much more laughable than Little Nell; she is also
much more of all that Little Nell was meant to be;
much more really devoted, pathetic, and brave. Dick
Swiveller is not only a much funnier fellow than Kit, he
is also a much more genuine fellow, being free from that
slight stain of "meekness," or the snobbishness of the re-
spectable poor, which the wise and perfect Chuckster
wisely and perfectly perceived in Kit. Susan Nipper is
not only more of a comic character than Florence; she
is more of a heroine than Florence any day of the week.
In "Our Mutual Friend" we do not, for some reason or
other, feel really very much excited about the fall or
rescue of Lizzie Hexam. She seems too romantic to be
really pathetic. But we do feel excited about the rescue
of Miss Lammle, because she is, like Toots, a holy fool;
because her pink nose and pink elbows, and candid out-
cry and open indecent affections do convey to us a sense of
innocence helpless among human dragons, of Androm-
eda tied naked to a rock. Dickens had to make a character humorous before he could make it human; it was
the only way he knew, and he ought to have always ad-
hered to it. Whether he knew it or not, the only two
really touching figures in "Martin Chuzzlewit" are the
Misses Pecksniff. Of the things he tried to treat unsmil-

136

ingly and grandly we can all make game to our heart's content. But when once he has laughed at a thing it is sacred for ever.

"Dombey," however, means first and foremost the finale of the early Dickens. It is difficult to say exactly in what it is that we perceive that the old crudity ends there, and does not reappear in "David Copperfield" or in any of the novels after it. But so certainly it is. In detached scenes and characters, indeed, Dickens kept up his farcical note almost or quite to the end. But this is the last farce; this is the last work in which a farcical license is tacitly claimed, a farcical note struck to start with. And in a sense his next novel may be called his first novel. But the growth of this great novel, "David Copperfield," is a thing very interesting, but at the same time very dark, for it is a growth in the soul. We have seen that Dickens's mind was in a stir of change; that he was dreaming of art, and even of realism. Hugely delighted as he invariably was with his own books, he was humble enough to be ambitious. He was even humble enough to be envious. In the matter of art, for instance, in the narrower sense, of arrangement and proportion in fictitious things, he began to be conscious of his deficiency, and even, in a stormy sort of way, ashamed of it; he tried to gain completeness even while raging at any one who called him incomplete. And in this matter of artistic construction, his ambition (and his success too) grew steadily up to the instant of his death. The end finds him attempting things that are at the opposite pole to the frank formlessness of "Pickwick." His last book, "The Mystery of Edwin Drood," depends entirely upon construction, even upon a centralized strategy. He staked everything upon a plot; he who had been the weakest of plotters, weaker than Sim Tappertit. He essayed a detective story, he who could never keep a secret; and he has kept it to this day. A new Dickens was really being born when Dickens died.

And as with art, so with reality. He wished to show that he could construct as well as anybody. He also wished to show that he could be as accurate as anybody. And in this connection (as in many others) we must recur constantly to the facts mentioned in connection with America and with his money-matters. We must recur, I mean, to the central fact that his desires were extravagant in quantity, but not in quality; that his wishes were excessive, but not eccentric. It must never be forgotten that sanity was his ideal, even when he seemed almost insane. It was thus with his literary aspirations. He was brilliant; but he wished sincerely to be solid. Nobody out of an asylum could deny that he was a genius and an unique writer; but he did not wish to be an unique writer, but an universal writer. Much of the manufactured pathos or rhetoric against which his enemies quite rightly rail, is really due to his desire to give all sides of life at once, to make his book a cosmos instead of a tale. He was sometimes really vulgar in his wish to be a literary Whiteley, an universal provider. Thus it was that he felt about realism and truth to life. Nothing is easier than to defend Dickens as Dickens, but Dickens wished to be everybody else. Nothing is easier than to defend Dickens's world as a fairyland, of which he alone has the key; to defend him as one defends Maeterlinck, or any other original writer. But Dickens was not content with being original, he had a wild wish to be true. He loved truth so much in the abstract that he sacrificed to the shadow of it his own glory. He denied his own divine originality, and pretended that he had plagiarized from life. He disowned his own soul's children, and said he had picked them up in the street.

And in this mixed and heated mood of anger and ambition, vanity and doubt, a new and great design was born. He loved to be romantic, yet he desired to be real. How if he wrote of a thing that was real and showed that it was romantic? He loved real life; but he also loved his own way. How if he wrote his own real life, but wrote it in his own way? How if he showed the carping critics who doubted the existence of his strange characters, his own yet stranger existence? How if he forced these pedants and unbelievers to admit that Weller and Pecksniff, Crummles and Swiveller, whom they thought so improbably wild and wonderful, were less wild and wonderful than Charles Dickens? What if he ended the quarrels about whether his romances could occur, by confessing that his romance had occurred?

For some time past, probably during the greater part of his life, he had made notes for an autobiography. I have already quoted an admirable passage from these notes, a passage reproduced in "David Copperfield," with little more alteration than a change of proper names—the passage which describes Captain Porter and the debtor's petition in the Marshalsea. But he probably perceived at last what a less keen intelligence must ultimately have perceived, that if an autobiography is really to be honest it must be turned into a work of fiction. If it is really to tell the truth, it must at all costs profess not to. No man dare say of himself, over his own name, how badly he has behaved. No man dare say of himself, over his own name, how well he has behaved. Moreover, of course a touch of fiction is almost always essential to the real conveying of fact, because fact, as experienced, has a fragmentariness which is bewildering at first hand and quite blinding at second hand. Facts have at least to be sorted into compartments and the proper head and tail given to each. The perfection and pointedness of art are a sort of substitute for the pungency of actuality. Without this selection and completion our life seems a tangle of unfinished tales, a heap of novels, all volume one. Dickens determined to make one complete novel of it.

For though there are many other aspects of "David Copperfield," this autobiographical aspect is, after all, the greatest. The point of the book is, that unlike all the other books of Dickens, it is concerned with quite common actualities, but it is concerned with them warmly and with the war-like sympathies. It is not only both realistic and romantic; it is realistic because it is romantic. It is human nature described with the human exaggeration. We all know the actual types in the book; they are not like the turgid and preternatural types elsewhere in Dickens. They are not purely poetic creations like Mr. Kenwiggs or Mr. Bunsby. We all know that they exist. We all know the stiff-necked and humorous old-fashioned nurse, so conventional and yet so original, so dependent and yet so independent. We all know the intrusive stepfather, the abstract strange male, coarse, handsome, sulky, successful; a breaker-up of homes. We all know the erect and sardonic spinster, the spinster who is so mad in small things and so sane in great ones. We all know the cock of the school; we all know Steerforth, the creature whom the gods love and even the servants respect. We know his poor and aristocratic mother, so proud, so gratified, so desolate. We know the Rosa Dartle type, the lonely woman in whom affection itself has stagnated into a sort of poison.

But while these are real characters they are real characters lit up with the colours of youth and passion. They are real people romantically felt; that is to say, they are real people felt as real people feel them. They are exaggerated, like all Dickens's figures: but they are not exaggerated as personalities are exaggerated by an artist; they are exaggerated as personalities are exaggerated by their own friends and enemies. The strong souls are seen through the glorious haze of the emotions that strong souls really create. We have Murdstone as he would be to a boy who hated him; and rightly, for a boy would hate him. We have Steerforth as he would be to a boy who adored him; and rightly, for a boy would adore him. It may be that if these persons had a mere terrestrial existence, they appeared to other eyes more insignificant. It may be that Murdstone in common life was only a heavy business man with a human side that David was too sulky to find. It may be that Steerforth was only an inch or two taller than David, and only a shade or two above him in the lower middle classes; but this does not make the book less true. In cataloguing the facts of life the author must not omit that massive fact, illusion.

When we say the book is true to life we must stipulate that it is especially true to youth; even to boyhood. All the characters seem a little larger than they really were, for David is looking up at them. And the early pages of the book are in particular astonishingly vivid. Parts of it seem like fragments of our forgotten infancy. The dark house of childhood, the loneliness, the things half understood, the nurse with her inscrutable sulks and her more inscrutable tenderness, the sudden deportations to distant places, the seaside and its childish friendships, all this stirs in us when we read it, like something out of a previous existence. Above all, Dickens has excellently depicted the child enthroned in that humble circle which only in after years he perceives to have been humble. Modern and cultured persons, I believe, object to their children seeing kitchen company or being taught by a woman like Peggotty. But surely it is more important to be educated in a sense of human dignity and equality than in anything else in the world. And a child who has once had to respect a kind and capable woman of the lower classes will respect the lower classes for ever. The true way to overcome the evil in class distinctions is not to denounce them as revolutionists denounce them, but to ignore them as children ignore them.

The early youth of David Copperfield is psychologically almost as good as his childhood. In one touch especially Dickens pierced the very core of the sensibility of boyhood; it was when he made David more afraid of a manservant than of anybody or anything else. The lowering Murdstone, the awful Mrs. Steerforth are not so alarming to him as Mr. Littimer, the unimpeachable gentleman's gentleman. This is exquisitely true to the masculine emotions, especially in their undeveloped state. A youth of common courage does not fear anything violent, but he is in mortal fear of anything correct. This may or may not be the reason that so few female writers understand their male characters, but this fact remains: that the more sincere and passionate and even headlong a lad is the more certain he is to be conventional. The bolder and freer he seems the more the traditions of the college or the rules of the club will hold him with their gyves of gossamer; and the less afraid he is of his enemies the more cravenly he will be afraid of his friends. Herein lies indeed the darkest peril of our ethical doubt and chaos. The fear is that as morals become less urgent, manners will become more so; and men who have forgotten the fear of God will retain the fear of Littimer. We shall merely sink into a much meaner bondage. For when you break the great laws, you do not get liberty; you do not even get anarchy. You get the small laws.

The sting and strength of this piece of fiction, then, do (by a rare accident) lie in the circumstance that it was so largely founded on fact. "David Copperfield" is the great answer of a great romancer to the realists. David says in effect: "What! you say that the Dickens tales are too purple really to have happened! Why, this is what happened to me, and it seemed the most purple of all. You say that the Dickens heroes are too handsome and triumphant! Why, no prince or paladin in Ariosto was ever so handsome and triumphant as the Head Boy seemed to me walking before me in the sun. You say the Dickens villains are too black! Why, there was no ink in the devil's ink-stand black enough for my own stepfather when I had to live in the same house with him. The facts are quite the other way to what you suppose. This life of grey studies and half tones, the absence of which you regret in Dickens, is only life as it is looked at. This life of heroes and villains is life as it is lived. The life a man knows best is exactly the life he finds most full of fierce certainties and battles between good and ill— his own. Oh, yes, the life we do not care about may easily be a psychological comedy. Other people's lives may easily be human documents. But a man's own life is always a melodrama."

There are other effective things in "David Copperfield"; they are not all autobiographical, but they nearly all have this new note of quietude and reality. Micawber is gigantic; an immense assertion of the truth that the way to live is to exaggerate everything. But of him I shall have to speak more fully in another connection. Mrs. Micawber, artistically speaking, is even better. She is very nearly the best thing in Dickens. Nothing could be more absurd, and at the same time more true, than her clear, argumentative manner of speech as she sits smiling and expounding in the midst of ruin. What could be more lucid and logical and unanswerable than her statement of the prolegomena of the Medway problem, of which the first step must be to "see the Medway," or of the coal-trade, which required talent and capital. "Talent Mr. Micawber has. Capital Mr. Micawber has not." It seems as if something should have come at last out of so clear and scientific an arrangement of ideas. Indeed if (as has been suggested) we regard "David Copperfield" as an unconscious defence of the poetic view of life, we might regard Mrs. Micawber as an unconscious satire on the logical view of life. She sits as a monument of the hopelessness and helplessness of reason in the face of this romantic and unreasonable world.

As I have taken "Dombey and Son" as the book before the transition, and "David Copperfield" as typical of the transition itself, I may perhaps take "Bleak House" as the book after the transition. "Bleak House" has every characteristic of his new realistic culture. Dickens never, as in his early books, revels now in the parts he likes and scamps the parts he does not, after the manner of Scott. He does not, as in previous tales, leave his heroes and heroines mere walking gentlemen and ladies with nothing at all to do but walk: he expends upon them at least ingenuity. By the expedients (successful or not) of the self-revelation of Esther or the humorous inconsistencies of Rick, he makes his younger figures if not lovable at least readable. Everywhere we see this tighter and more careful grip. He does not, for instance, when he wishes to denounce a dark institution, sandwich it in as a mere episode in a rambling story of adventure, as the debtor's prison is embedded in the body of Pickwick or the low Yorkshire school in the body of Nicholas Nickleby. He puts the Court of Chancery in the centre of the stage, a sombre and sinister temple, and groups round it in artistic relation decaying and fantastic figures, its offspring and its satirists. An old dipsomaniac keeps a rag and bone shop, type of futility and antiquity, and calls himself the Lord Chancellor. A little mad old maid hangs about the courts on a forgotten or imaginary lawsuit, and says with perfect and pungent irony, "I am expecting a judgment shortly, on the Day of Judgment." Rick and Ada and Esther are not mere strollers who have strayed into the court of law, they are its children, its symbols, and its victims. The righteous indignation of the book is not at the red heat of anarchy, but at the white heat of art. Its anger is patient and plodding, like some historic revenge. Moreover, it slowly and carefully creates the real psychology of oppression. The endless formality, the endless unemotional urbanity, the endless hope deferred, these things make one feel the fact of injustice more than the madness of Nero. For it is not the activeness of tyranny that maddens, but its passiveness. We hate the deafness of the god more than his strength. Silence is the unbearable repartee.

Again we can see in this book strong traces of an increase in social experience. Dickens, as his fame carried him into more fashionable circles, began really to understand something of what is strong and what is weak in the English upper class. Sir Leicester Deadlock is a far more effective condemnation of oligarchy than the ugly swagger of Sir Mulberry Hawk, because pride stands out more plainly in all its impotence and insolence as the one weakness of a good man, than as one of the million weaknesses of a bad one. Dickens, like all young Radicals, had imagined in his youth that aristocracy rested upon the hardness of somebody; he found, as we all do, that it rests upon the softness of everybody. It is very hard not to like Sir Leicester Deadlock, not to applaud his silly old speeches, so foolish, so manly, so genuinely English, so disastrous to England. It is true that the English people love a lord, but it is not true that they fear him; rather, if anything, they pity him; there creeps into their love something of the feeling they have towards a baby or a black man. In their hearts they think it admirable that Sir Leicester Deadlock should be able to speak at all. And so a system, which no iron laws and no bloody battles could possibly force upon a people, is preserved from generation to generation by pure, weak good-nature.

In "Bleak House" occurs the character of Harold Skimpole, the character whose alleged likeness to Leigh Hunt has laid Dickens open to so much disapproval. Unjust disapproval, I think, as far as fundamental morals are concerned. In method he was a little clamorous and clumsy, as, indeed, he was apt to be. But when he said that it was possible to combine a certain tone of conversation taken from a particular man with other characteristics which were not meant to be his, he surely said what all men who write stories know. A work of fiction often consists in combining a pair of whiskers seen in one street with a crime seen in another. He may quite possibly have really meant only to make Leigh Hunt's light philosophy the mask for a new kind of scamp, as a variant on the pious mask of Pecksniff or the candid mask of Bagstock. He may never once have had the unfriendly thought, "Suppose Hunt behaved like a rascal!" he may have only had the fanciful thought, "Suppose a rascal behaved like Hunt!"

But there is a good reason for mentioning Skimpole especially. In the character of Skimpole, Dickens displayed again a quality that was very admirable in him—I mean a disposition to see things sanely and to satirize even his own faults. He was commonly occupied in satirizing the Gradgrinds, the economists, the men of

Smiles and Self-Help. For him there was nothing poorer than their wealth, nothing more selfish than their self-denial. And against them he was in the habit of pitting the people of a more expansive habit—the happy Swivellers and Micawbers, who, if they were poor, were at least as rich as their last penny could make them. He loved that great Christian carelessness that seeks its meat from God. It was merely a kind of uncontrollable honesty that forced him into urging the other side. He could not disguise from himself or from the world that the man who began by seeking his meat from God might end by seeking his meat from his neighbour, without apprising his neighbour of the fact. He had shown how good irresponsibility could be; he could not stoop to hide how bad it could be. He created Skimpole; and Skimpole is the dark underside of Micawber.

In attempting Skimpole he attempted something with a great and urgent meaning. He attempted it, I say; I do not assert that he carried it through. As has been remarked, he was never successful in describing psychological change; his characters are the same yesterday, to-day, and for ever. And critics have complained very justly of the crude villainy of Skimpole's action in the matter of Joe and Mr. Bucket. Certainly Skimpole had no need to commit a clumsy treachery to win a clumsy bribe; he had only to call on Mr. Jarndyce. He had lost his honour too long to need to sell it.

The effect is bad; but I repeat that the aim was great. Dickens wished, under the symbol of Skimpole, to point out a truth which is perhaps the most terrible in moral psychology. I mean the fact that it is by no means easy to draw the line between light and heavy offence. He desired to show that there are no faults, however kindly, that we can afford to flatter or to let alone; he meant that perhaps Skimpole had once been as good a man as

Swiveller. If flattered or let alone, our kindliest fault can destroy our kindliest virtue. A thing may begin as a very human weakness, and end as a very inhuman weakness. Skimpole means that the extremes of evil are much nearer than we think. A man may begin by being too generous to pay his debts, and end by being too mean to pay his debts. For the vices are very strangely in league, and encourage each other. A sober man may become a drunkard through being a coward. A brave man may become a coward through being a drunkard. That is the thing Dickens was darkly trying to convey in Skimpole —that a man might become a mountain of selfishness if he attended only to the Dickens virtues. There is nothing that can be neglected; there is no such thing (he meant) as a peccadillo.

I have dwelt on this consciousness of his because, alas, it had a very sharp edge for himself. Even while he was permitting a fault, originally small, to make a comedy of Skimpole, a fault, originally small, was making a tragedy of Charles Dickens. For Dickens also had a bad quality, not intrinsically very terrible, which he allowed to wreck his life. He also had a small weakness that could sometimes become stronger than all his strengths. His selfishness was not, it need hardly be said, the selfishness of Gradgrind; he was particularly compassionate and liberal. Nor was it in the least the selfishness of Skimpole. He was entirely self-dependent, industrious, and dignified. His selfishness was wholly a selfishness of the nerves. Whatever his whim or the temperature of the instant told him to do, must be done. He was the type of man who would break a window if it would not open and give him air. And this weakness of his had, by the time of which we speak, led to a breach between himself and his wife which he was too exasperated and excited to heal in time. Everything must be put right,

148

and put right at once, with him. If London bored him, he must go to the Continent at once; if the Continent bored him, he must come back to London at once. If the day was too noisy, the whole household must be quiet; if night was too quiet, the whole household must wake up. Above all, he had this supreme character of the domestic despot—that his good temper was, if possible, more despotic than his bad temper. When he was miserable (as he often was, poor fellow), they only had to listen to his railings. When he was happy they had to listen to his novels. All this, which was mainly mere excitability, did not seem to amount to much; it did not in the least mean that he had ceased to be a clean-living and kind-hearted and quite honest man. But there was this evil about it—that he did not resist his little weakness at all; he pampered it as Skimpole pampered his. And it separated him and his wife. A mere silly trick of temperament did everything that the blackest misconduct could have done. A random sensibility, started about the shuffling of papers or the shutting of a window, ended by tearing two clean, Christian people from each other, like a blast of bigamy or adultery.

CHAPTER IX

Later Life and Works

I HAVE deliberately in this book mentioned only such facts in the life of Dickens as were, I will not say significant (for all facts must be significant, including the million facts that can never be mentioned by anybody), but such facts as illustrated my own immediate meaning. I have observed this method consistently and without shame because I think that we can hardly make too evident a chasm between books which profess to be statements of all ascertainable facts, and books which (like this one) profess only to contain a particular opinion or a summary deducible from the facts. Books like Forster's exhaustive work and others exist, and are as accessible as St. Paul's Cathedral; we have them in common as we have the facts of the physical universe; and it seems highly desirable that the function of making an exhaustive catalogue and that of making an individual generalization should not be confused. No catalogue, of course, can contain all the facts even of five minutes; every catalogue, however long and learned, must be not only a bold, but, one may say, an audacious selection. But if a great many facts are given, the reader gains a blurred belief that all the facts are being given. In a professedly personal judgment it is therefore clearer and more honest to give only a few illustrative facts, leaving the other obtainable facts to balance them. For thus it is made quite clear that the thing is a sketch, an affair of a few lines.

It is as well, however, to make at this point a pause sufficient to indicate the main course of the later life of the novelist. And it is best to begin with the man himself, as he appeared in those last days of popularity and public distinction. Many are still alive who remember him in his after-dinner speeches, his lectures, and his many public activities; as I am not one of these, I cannot correct my notions with that flash of the living features without which a description may be subtly and entirely wrong. Once a man is dead, if it be only yesterday, the newcomer must piece him together from descriptions really as much at random as if he were describing Cæsar or Henry II. Allowing, however, for this inevitable falsity, a figure vivid and a little fantastic, does walk across the stage of Forster's "Life."

Dickens was of a middle size and his vivacity and relative physical insignificance probably gave rather the impression of small size; certainly of the absence of bulk. In early life he wore, even for that epoch, extravagant clusters of brown hair, and in later years, a brown moustache and a fringe of brown beard (cut like a sort of broad and bushy imperial) sufficiently individual in shape to give him a faint air as of a foreigner. His face had a peculiar tint or quality which is hard to describe even after one has contrived to imagine it. It was the quality which Mrs. Carlyle felt to be, as it were, metallic, and compared to clear steel. It was, I think, a sort of pale glitter and animation, very much alive and yet with something deathly about it, like a corpse galvanized by a god. His face (if this was so) was curiously a counterpart of his character. For the essence of Dickens's character was that it was at once tremulous and yet hard and sharp, just as the bright blade of a sword is tremulous and yet hard and sharp. He vibrated at every touch and yet he was indestructible; you could bend him, but you could not break him. Brown of hair and beard, somewhat pale of visage (especially in his later days of excitement and ill-health) he had quite exceptionally bright and active eyes; eyes that were always darting about like brilliant birds to pick up all the tiny things of which he made more, perhaps, than any novelist has done; for he was a sort of poetical Sherlock Holmes. The mouth behind the brown beard was large and mobile, like the mouth of an actor; indeed he was an actor, in many things too much of an actor. In his lectures, in later years, he could turn his strange face into any of the innumerable mad masks that were the faces of his grotesque characters. He could make his face fall suddenly into the blank inanity of Mrs. Raddle's servant, or swell, as if to twice its size, into the apoplectic energy of Mr. Serjeant Buzfuz. But the outline of his face itself, from his youth upwards, was cut quite delicate and decisive, and in repose and its own keen way, may even have looked effeminate.

The dress of the comfortable classes during the later years of Dickens was, compared with ours, somewhat slipshod and somewhat gaudy. It was the time of loose pegtop trousers of an almost Turkish oddity, of large ties, of loose short jackets and of loose long whiskers. Yet even this expansive period, it must be confessed, considered Dickens a little too flashy or, as some put it, too Frenchified in his dress. He wore velvet coats; he wore wild waistcoats that were like incredible sunsets; he wore large hats of an unnecessary and startling whiteness. He did not mind being seen in sensational dress-ing-gowns; nay, he had his portrait painted in one of them. All this is not meritorious; neither is it particularly discreditable; it is a characteristic only, but an important one. He was an absolutely independent and entirely self-respecting man. But he had none of that old dusty, half-dignified English feeling upon which Thackeray was so sensitive; I mean the desire to be regarded as a private gentleman, which means at bottom the desire to be left alone. This again is not a merit; it is only one of the milder aspects of aristocracy. But meritorious or not, Dickens did not possess it. He had no objection to being stared at, if he were also admired. He did not exactly pose in the oriental manner of Disraeli; his instincts were too clean for that; but he did pose somewhat in the French manner, of some leaders like Mirabeau and Gambetta. Nor had he the dull desire to "get on" which makes men die contented as inarticulate Under Secretaries of State. He did not desire success so much as fame, the old human glory, the applause and wonder of the people. Such he was as he walked down the street in his white hat, probably with a slight swagger.

His private life consisted of one tragedy and ten thousand comedies. By one tragedy I mean one real and rending moral tragedy—the failure of his marriage. He loved his children dearly, and more than one of them died; but in sorrows like these there is no violence and above all no shame. The end of life is not tragic like the end of love. And by the ten thousand comedies I mean the whole texture of his life, his letters, his conversation, which were one incessant carnival of insane and inspired improvisation. So far as he could prevent it, he never permitted a day of his life to be ordinary. There was always some prank, some impetuous proposal, some practical joke, some sudden hospitality, some sudden disappearance. It is related of him (I give one anecdote out of a hundred) that in his last visit to America, when he was already reeling as it were under the blow that was to be mortal, he remarked quite casually to his companions that a row of painted cottages looked exactly like the painted shops in a pantomime. No sooner had the suggestion passed his lips than he leapt at the nearest doorway and in exact imitation of the clown in the harlequinade, beat conscientiously with his fist, not on the door (for that would have burst the canvas scenery of course), but on the side of the doorpost. Having done this he lay down ceremoniously across the doorstep for the owner to fall over him if he should come rushing out. He then got up gravely and went on his way. His whole life was full of such unexpected energies, precisely like those of the pantomime clown. Dickens had indeed a great and fundamental affinity with the landscape, or rather house-scape, of the harlequinade. He liked high houses, and sloping roofs, and deep areas. But he would have been really happy if some good fairy of the eternal pantomime had given him the power of flying off the roofs and pitching harmlessly down the height of the houses and bounding out of the areas like an indiarubber ball. The divine lunatic in "Nicholas Nickleby" comes nearest to his dream. I really think Dickens would rather have been that one of his characters than any of the others. With what excitement he would have struggled down the chimney. With what ecstatic energy he would have hurled the cucumbers over the garden wall.

His letters exhibit even more the same incessant creative force. His letters are as creative as any of his literary creations. His shortest postcard is often as good as his ablest novel; each one of them is spontaneous; each one of them is different. He varies even the form and shape of the letter as far as possible; now it is in absurd French! now it is from one of his characters; now it is an advertisement for himself as a stray dog. All of them are very funny; they are not only very funny, but they are quite as funny as his finished and published work. This is the ultimately amazing thing about Dickens; the amount there is of him. He wrote, at the very least, sixteen thick important books packed full of original creation. And if you had burnt them all he could have written sixteen more, as a man writes idle letters to his friend.

In connection with this exuberant part of his nature there is another thing to be noted, if we are to make a personal picture of him. Many modern people, chiefly women, have been heard to object to the Bacchic element in the books of Dickens, that celebration of social drinking as a supreme symbol of social living, which those books share with almost all the great literature of mankind, including the New Testament. Undoubtedly there is an abnormal amount of drinking in a page of Dickens, as there is an abnormal amount of fighting, say, in a page of Dumas. If you reckon up the beers and brandies of Mr. Bob Sawyer, with the care of an arithmetician and the deductions of a pathologist, they rise alarmingly, like a rising tide at sea. Dickens did defend drink clamorously, praised it with passion, and described whole orgies of it with enormous gusto. Yet it is wonderfully typical of his prompt and impatient nature that he himself drank comparatively little. He was the type of man who could be so eager in praising the cup that he left the cup untasted. It was a part of his active and feverish temperament that he did not drink wine very much. But it was a part of his humane philosophy, of his religion, that he did drink wine. To healthy European philosophy, wine is a symbol; to European religion it is a sacrament. Dickens approved it because it was a great human institution, one of the rites of civilization, and this it certainly is. The teetotaller who stands outside it may have perfectly clear ethical reasons of his own, as a man may have who stands outside education or nationality, who refuses to go to an University or to serve in an Army. But he is neglecting one of the great social things that man has added to nature. The teetotaller has chosen a most unfortunate phrase for the drunkard when he says that the drunkard is making a beast of himself. The man who drinks ordinarily makes nothing but an ordinary man of himself. The man who drinks excessively makes a devil of himself. But nothing connected with a human and artistic thing like wine can bring one nearer to the brute life of nature. The only man who is, in the exact and literal sense of the words, making a beast of himself is the teetotaller.

The tone of Dickens towards religion, though like that of most of his contemporaries, philosophically disturbed and rather historically ignorant, had an element that was very characteristic of himself. He had all the prejudices of his time. He had, for instance, that dislike of defined dogmas, which really means a preference for unexamined dogmas. He had the usual vague notion that the whole of our human past was packed with nothing but insane Tories. He had, in a word, all the old Radical ignorances which went along with the old Radical acuteness and courage and public spirit. But this spirit tended, in almost all the others who held it, to a specific dislike of the Church of England; and a disposition to set the other sects against it, as truer types of inquiry, or of individualism. Dickens had a definite tenderness for the Church of England. He might have even called it a weakness for the Church of England, but he had it. Something in those placid services, something in that reticent and humane liturgy pleased him against all the tendencies of his time; pleased him in the best part of himself, his virile love of charity and peace. Once, in a puff of anger at the Church's political stupidity (which is indeed profound), he left it for a week or two and went to an Unitarian Chapel; in a week or two he came back. This curious and sentimental hold of the English Church upon him increased with years. In the book he was at work on when he died he describes the Minor Canon, humble, chivalrous, tender-hearted, answering with indignant simplicity the froth and platform righteousness of the sectarian philanthropist. He upholds Canon Crisparkle and satirizes Mr. Honeythunder. Almost every one of the other Radicals, his friends, would have upheld Mr. Honeythunder and satirized Canon Crisparkle.

I have mentioned this matter for a special reason. It brings us back to that apparent contradiction or dualism in Dickens to which, in one connection or another, I have often adverted, and which, in one shape or another, constitutes the whole crux of his character. I mean the union of a general wildness approaching lunacy, with a sort of secret moderation almost amounting to mediocrity. Dickens was, more or less, the man I have described—sensitive, theatrical, amazing, a bit of a dandy, a bit of a buffoon. Nor are such characteristics, whether weak or wild, entirely accidents or externals. He had some false theatrical tendencies integral in his nature. For instance, he had one most unfortunate habit, a habit that often put him in the wrong, even when he happened to be in the right. He had an incurable habit of explaining himself. This reduced his admirers to the mental condition of the authentic but hitherto uncelebrated little girl who said to her mother,

"I think I should understand if only you wouldn't ex-plain." Dickens always would explain. It was a part of that instinctive publicity of his which made him at once a splendid democrat and a little too much of an actor. He carried it to the craziest lengths. He actually wanted to have printed in *Punch,* it is said, an apology for his own action in the matter of his marriage. That incident alone is enough to suggest that his external offers and pro-posals were sometimes like screams heard from Bedlam. Yet it remains true that he had in him a central part that was pleased only by the most decent and the most reposeful rites, by things of which the Anglican prayer-book is very typical. It is certainly true that he was often extravagant. It is most certainly equally true that he detested and despised extravagance.

The best explanation can be found in his literary genius. His literary genius consisted in a contradictory capacity at once to entertain and to deride—very ridic-ulous ideas. If he is a buffoon, he is laughing at buf-foonery. His books were in some ways the wildest on the face of the world. Rabelais did not introduce into Paphlagonia or the Kingdom of the Coqcigrues satiric figures more frantic and misshapen than Dickens made to walk about the Strand and Lincoln's Inn. But for all that, you come, in the core of him, on a sudden quie-tude and good sense. Such, I think, was the core of Rabelais, such were all the far-stretching and violent satirists. This is a point essential to Dickens, though very little comprehended in our current tone of thought. Dickens was an immoderate jester, but a moderate thinker. He was an immoderate jester because he was a moderate thinker. What we moderns call the wildness of his imagination was actually created by what we mod-erns call the tameness of his thought. I mean that he felt the full insanity of all extreme tendencies, because he was himself so sane; he felt eccentricities, because he was in the centre. We are always, in these days, asking our violent prophets to write violent satires; but violent prophets can never possibly write violent satires. In order to write satire like that of Rabelais—satire that juggles with the stars and kicks the world about like a football—it is necessary to be one's self temperate, and even mild. A modern man like Nietzsche, a modern man like Gorky, a modern man like d'Annunzio, could not possibly write real and riotous satire. They are themselves too much on the borderlands. They could not be a success as caricaturists, for they are already a great success as caricatures.

I have mentioned his religious preference merely as an instance of this interior moderation. To say, as some have done, that he attacked Nonconformity is quite a false way of putting it. It is clean across the whole trend of the man and his time to suppose that he could have felt bitterness against any theological body as a theological body; but anything like religious extravagance, whether Protestant or Catholic, moved him to an extravagance of satire. And he flung himself into the drunken energy of Stiggins, he piled up to the stars the "verbose flights of stairs" of Mr. Chadband, exactly because his own conception of religion was the quiet and impersonal Morning Prayer. It is typical of him that he had a peculiar hatred for speeches at the graveside.

An even clearer case of what I mean can be found in his political attitude. He seemed to some an almost anarchic satirist. He made equal fun of the systems which reformers made war on, and of the instruments on which reformers relied. He made no secret of his feeling that the average English premier was an accidental ass. In two superb sentences he summed up and swept away the whole British constitution: "England, for the last week, has been in an awful state. Lord Coodle would go out, Sir Thomas Doodle wouldn't come in, and there being no people in England to speak of except Coodle and Doodle, the country has been without a government." He lumped all cabinets and all government offices together, and made the same game of them all. He created his most staggering humbugs, his most adorable and incredible idiots, and set them on the highest thrones of our national system. To many moderate and progressive people, such a satirist seemed to be insulting heaven and earth, ready to wreck society for some mad alternative, prepared to pull down St. Paul's, and on its ruins erect a gory guillotine. Yet, as a matter of fact, this apparent wildness of his came from his being, if anything, a very moderate politician. It came, not at all from fanaticism, but from a rather rational detachment. He had the sense to see that the British constitution was not democracy, but the British constitution. It was an artificial system—like any other, good in some ways, bad in others. His satire of it sounded wild to those that worshipped it; but his satire of it arose not from his having any wild enthusiasm against it, but simply from his not having, like every one else, a wild enthusiasm for it. Alone, as far as I know, among all the great Englishmen of that age, he realized the thing that Frenchmen and Irishmen understand. I mean the fact that popular government is one thing, and representative government another. He realized that representative government has many minor disadvantages, one of them being that it is never representative. He speaks of his "hope to have made every man in England feel something of the contempt for the House of Commons that I have." He says also these two things, both of which are wonderfully penetrating as coming from a good Radical in 1855, for they contain a perfect statement of the peril in which we now stand, and which may, if it please God, sting us into avoiding the long vista at the end of which one sees so clearly the dignity and the decay of Venice—

"I am hourly strengthened," he says, "in my old belief, that our political aristocracy and our tuft-hunting are the death of England. In all this business I don't see a gleam of hope. As to the popular spirit, it has come to be so entirely separated from the Parliament and the Government, and so perfectly apathetic about them both, that I seriously think it a most portentous sign." And he says also this: "I really am serious in thinking— and I have given as painful consideration to the subject as a man with children to live and suffer after him can possibly give it—that representative government is become altogether a failure with us, that the English gentilities and subserviences render the people unfit for it, and the whole thing has broken down since the great seventeenth century time, and has no hope in it."

These are the words of a wise and perhaps melancholy man, but certainly not of an unduly excited one. It is worth noting, for instance, how much more directly Dickens goes to the point than Carlyle did, who noted many of the same evils. But Carlyle fancied that our modern English government was wordy and long-winded because it was democratic government. Dickens saw, what is certainly the fact, that it is wordy and long-winded because it is aristocratic government, the two most pleasant aristocratic qualities being a love of literature and an unconsciousness of time. But all this amounts to the same conclusion of the matter. Frantic figures like Stiggins and Chadband were created out of the quietude of his religious preference. Wild creations like the Barnacles and the Bounderbys were produced in a kind of ecstasy of the ordinary, of the obvious in political justice. His monsters were made out of his level and his moderation, as the old monsters were made out of the level sea.

Such was the man of genius we must try to imagine; violently emotional, yet with a good judgment; pugnacious, but only when he thought himself oppressed; prone to think himself oppressed, yet not cynical about human motives. He was a man remarkably hard to understand or to reanimate. He almost always had reasons for his action; his error was that he always expounded them. Sometimes his nerve snapped; and then he was mad. Unless it did so he was quite unusually sane.

Such a rough sketch at least must suffice us in order to summarize his later years. Those years were occupied, of course, in two main additions to his previous activities. The first was the series of public readings and lectures which he now began to give systematically. The second was his successive editorship of *Household Words* and of *All the Year Round*. He was of a type that enjoys every new function and opportunity. He had been so many things in his life, a reporter, an actor, a conjurer, a poet. As he had enjoyed them all, so he enjoyed being a lecturer, and enjoyed being an editor. It is certain that his audiences (who sometimes stacked themselves so thick that they lay flat on the platform all round him) enjoyed his being a lecturer. It is not so certain that the sub-editors enjoyed his being an editor. But in both connections the main matter of importance is the effect on the permanent work of Dickens himself. The readings were important for this reason, that they fixed, as if by some public and pontifical pronouncement, what was Dickens's interpretation of Dickens's work. Such a knowledge is mere tradition, but it is very forcible. My own family has handed on to me, and I shall probably hand on to the next generation, a definite memory of how Dickens made his face suddenly like the face of an idiot in impersonating Mrs. Raddle's servant, Betsy. This does serve one of the permanent purposes of tradition; it does make it a little more difficult for any ingenious person to prove that Betsy was meant to be a brilliant satire on the over-cultivation of the intellect.

As for his relation to his two magazines, it is chiefly important, first for the admirable things that he wrote in the magazines himself (one cannot forbear to mention the inimitable monologue of the waiter in "Somebody's Luggage"), and secondly for the fact that in his capacity of editor he made one valuable discovery. He discovered Wilkie Collins. Wilkie Collins was the one man of unmistakable genius who has a certain affinity with Dickens; an affinity in this respect, that they both combine in a curious way a modern and cockney and even commonplace opinion about things with a huge elemental sympathy with strange oracles and spirits and old night. There were no two men in Mid-Victorian England, with their top-hats and umbrellas, more typical of its rationality and dull reform; and there were no two men who could touch them at a ghost story. No two men would have more contempt for superstitions; and no two men could so create the superstitious thrill. Indeed, our modern mystics make a mistake when they wear long hair or loose ties to attract the spirits. The elves and the old gods when they revisit the earth really go straight for a dull top-hat. For it means simplicity, which the gods love.

Meanwhile his books, which, as brilliant as ever, were appearing from time to time, bore witness to that increasing tendency to a more careful and responsible treatment which we have marked in the transition which culminated in "Bleak House." His next important book, "Hard Times," strikes an almost unexpected note of severity. The characters are indeed exaggerated, but they are bitterly and deliberately exaggerated; they are not exaggerated with the old unconscious high spirits of Nicholas Nickleby or Martin Chuzzlewit. Dickens exaggerates Bounderby because he really hates him. He exaggerated Pecksniff because he really loved him. "Hard Times" is not one of the greatest books of Dickens; but it is perhaps in a sense one of his greatest monuments. It stamps and records the reality of Dickens's emotion on a great many things that were then considered unphilosophical grumblings, but which since have swelled into the immense phenomenon of the Socialist philosophy. To call Dickens a Socialist is a wild exaggeration; but the truth and peculiarity of his position might be expressed thus: that even when everybody thought that Liberalism meant individualism he was emphatically a Liberal and emphatically not an individualist. Or the truth might be better still stated in this manner: that he saw that there was a secret thing, called humanity, to which both extreme Socialism and extreme individualism were profoundly and inexpressibly indifferent, and that this permanent and presiding humanity was the thing he happened to understand; he knew that individualism is nothing and non-individualism is nothing but the keeping of the commandment of man. He felt, as a novelist should, that the question is too much discussed as to whether a man is in favour of this or that scientific philosophy; that there is another question, whether the scientific philosophy is in favour of the man. That is why such books as "Hard Times" will remain always a part of the power and tradition of Dickens. He saw that economic systems are not things like the stars, but things like the lamp-posts, manifestations of the human mind, and things to be judged by the human heart.

164

Thenceforward until the end his books grow consistently graver and, as it were, more responsible; he improves as an artist if not always as a creator. "Little Dorrit" (published in 1857) is at once in some ways so much more subtle and in every way so much more sad than the rest of his work that it bores Dickensians and especially pleases George Gissing. It is the only one of the Dickens tales which could please Gissing, not only by its genius, but also by its atmosphere. There is something a little modern and a little sad, something also out of tune with the main trend of Dickens's moral feeling, about the description of the character of Dorrit as actually and finally weakened by his wasting experiences, as not lifting any cry above the conquered years. It is but a faint fleck of shadow. But the illimitable white light of human hopefulness, of which I spoke at the beginning, is ebbing away, the work of the Revolution is growing weaker everywhere; and the night of necessitarianism cometh when no man can work. For the first time in a book by Dickens perhaps we really do feel that the hero is forty-five. Clennam is certainly very much older than Mr. Pickwick.

This was indeed only a fugitive grey cloud; he went on to breezier operations. But whatever they were, they still had the note of the later days. They have a more cautious craftsmanship; they have a more mellow and a more mixed human sentiment. Shadows fell upon his page from the other and sadder figures out of the Victorian decline. A good instance of this is his next book, "A Tale of Two Cities" (1859). In dignity and eloquence it almost stands alone among the books by Dickens, but it also stands alone among his books in this respect, that it is not entirely by Dickens. It owes its inspiration avowedly to the passionate and cloudy pages of Carlyle's "French Revolution." And there is something quite essentially inconsistent between Carlyle's disturbed and half-sceptical transcendentalism and the original school and spirit to which Dickens belonged, the lucid and laughing decisiveness of the old convinced and contented Radicalism. Hence the genius of Dickens cannot save him, just as the great genius of Carlyle could not save him from making a picture of the French Revolution, which was delicately and yet deeply erroneous. Both tend too much to represent it as a mere elemental outbreak of hunger or vengeance; they do not see enough that it was a war for intellectual principles, even for intellectual platitudes. We, the modern English, cannot easily understand the French Revolution, because we cannot easily understand the idea of bloody battle for pure common sense; we cannot understand common sense in arms and conquering. In modern England common sense appears to mean putting up with existing conditions. For us a practical politician really means a man who can be thoroughly trusted to do nothing at all; that is where his practicality comes in. The French feeling—the feeling at the back of the Revolution—was that the more sensible a man was, the more you must look out for slaughter.

In all the imitators of Carlyle, including Dickens, there is an obscure sentiment that the thing for which the Frenchmen died must have been something new and queer, a paradox, a strange idolatry. But when such blood ran in the streets, it was for the sake of a truism; when those cities were shaken to their foundations, they were shaken to their foundations by a truism.

I have mentioned this historical matter because it illustrates these later and more mingled influences which at once improve and as it were perplex the later work of Dickens. For Dickens had in his original mental composition capacities for understanding this cheery

166

and sensible element in the French Revolution far better than Carlyle. The French Revolution was, among other things, French, and, so far as that goes, could never have a precise counterpart in so jolly and autochthonous an Englishman as Charles Dickens. But there was a great deal of the actual and unbroken tradition of the Revolution itself in his early Radical indictments; in his denunciations of the Fleet Prison there was a great deal of the capture of the Bastille. There was, above all, a certain reasonable impatience which was the essence of the old Republican, and which is quite unknown to the Revolutionist in modern Europe. The old Radical did not feel exactly that he was "in revolt"; he felt if anything that a number of idiotic institutions had revolted against reason and against him. Dickens, I say, had the revolutionary idea, though an English form of it, by clear and conscious inheritance; Carlyle had to rediscover the Revolution by a violence of genius and vision. If Dickens, then, took from Carlyle (as he said he did) his image of the Revolution, it does certainly mean that he had forgotten something of his own youth and come under the more complex influences of the end of the nineteenth century. His old hilarious and sentimental view of human nature seems for a moment dimmed in "Little Dorrit." His old political simplicity has been slightly disturbed by Carlyle.

I repeat that this graver note is varied, but it remains a graver note. We see it struck, I think, with particular and remarkable success in "Great Expectations" (1860–61). This fine story is told with a consistency and quietude of individuality which is rare in Dickens. But so far had he travelled along the road of a heavier reality, that he even intended to give the tale an unhappy ending, making Pip lose Estella for ever; and he was only dissuaded from it by the robust romanticism of Bulwer-

Lytton. But the best part of the tale—the account of the vacillations of the hero between the humble life to which he owes everything, and the gorgeous life from which he expects something—touches a very true and somewhat tragic part of morals; for the great paradox of morality (the paradox to which only the religions have given an adequate expression) is that the very vilest kind of fault is exactly the most easy kind. We read in books and ballads about the wild fellow who might kill a man or smoke opium, but who would never stoop to lying or cowardice or to "anything mean." But for actual human beings opium and slaughter have only occasional charm; the permanent human temptation is the temptation to be mean. The one standing probability is the probability of becoming a cowardly hypocrite. The circle of the traitors is the lowest of the abyss, and it is also the easiest to fall into. That is one of the ringing realities of the Bible, that it does not make its great men commit grand sins; it makes its great men (such as David and St. Peter) commit small sins and behave like sneaks.

Dickens has dealt with this easy descent of desertion, this silent treason, with remarkable accuracy in the account of the indecisions of Pip. It contains a good suggestion of that weak romance which is the root of all snobbishness: that the mystery which belongs to patrician life excites us more than the open, even the indecent virtues of the humble. Pip is keener about Miss Havisham, who may mean well by him, than about Joe Gargery, who evidently does. All this is very strong and wholesome; but it is still a little stern. "Our Mutual Friend" (1864) brings us back a little into his merrier and more normal manner; some of the satire, such as that upon Veneering's election, is in the best of his old style, so airy and fanciful, yet hitting so suddenly and so hard. But even here we find the fuller and more serious treatment of psychology; notably in the two facts that he creates a really human villain, Bradley Headstone, and also one whom we might call a really human hero, Eugene, if it were not that he is much too human to be called a hero at all. It has been said (invariably by cads) that Dickens never described a gentleman; it is like saying that he never described a zebra. A gentleman is a very rare animal among human creatures, and to people like Dickens, interested in all humanity, not a supremely important one. But in Eugene Wrayburne he does, whether consciously or not, turn that accusation with a vengeance. For he not only describes a gentleman but describes the inner weakness and peril that belong to a gentleman, the devil that is always rending the entrails of an idle and agreeable man. In Eugene's purposeless pursuit of Lizzie Hexam, in his yet more purposeless torturing of Bradley Headstone, the author has marvellously realized that singular empty obstinacy that drives the whims and pleasures of a leisured class. He sees that there is nothing that such a man more stubbornly adheres to, than the thing that he does not particularly want to do. We are still in serious psychology.

His last book represents yet another new departure, dividing him from the chaotic Dickens of days long before. His last book is not merely an attempt to improve his power of construction in a story: it is an attempt to rely entirely on that power of construction. It not only has a plot, it is a plot. "The Mystery of Edwin Drood" (1870) was in such a sense, perhaps, the most ambitious book that Dickens ever attempted. It is, as every one knows, a detective story, and certainly a very successful one, as is attested by the tumult of discussion as to its proper solution. In this, quite apart from its unfinished state, it stands, I think, alone among the author's works. Elsewhere, if he introduced a mystery, he seldom took the trouble to make it very mysterious. "Our Mutual Friend" was finished, but if only half of it were readable, I think any one could see that John Rokesmith was John Harman. "Bleak House" is finished, but if it were only half finished I think any one would guess that Lady Deadlock and Nemo had sinned in the past. "Edwin Drood" is not finished; for in the very middle of it Dickens died.

He had altogether overstrained himself in a last lecturing tour in America. He was a man in whom any serious malady would naturally make very rapid strides; for he had the temper of an irrational invalid. I have said before that there was in his curious character something that was feminine. Certainly there was nothing more entirely feminine than this, that he worked because he was tired. Fatigue bred in him a false and feverish industry, and his case increased, like the case of a man who drinks to cure the effects of drink. He died in 1870; and the whole nation mourned him as no public man has ever been mourned; for prime ministers and princes were private persons compared with Dickens. He had been a great popular king, like a king of some more primal age whom his people could come and see, giving judgment under an oak tree. He had in essence held great audiences of millions, and made proclamations to more than one of the nations of the earth. His obvious omnipresence in every part of public life was like the omnipresence of the sovereign. His secret omnipresence in every house and hut of private life was more like the omnipresence of a deity. Compared with that popular leadership all the fusses of the last forty years are diversions in idleness. Compared with such a case as his it may be said that we play with our politicians, and manage to endure our authors. We shall never have again such a popularity until we have again a people.

He left behind him this almost sombre fragment, "The Mystery of Edwin Drood." As one turns it over the tragic element of its truncation mingles somewhat with an element of tragedy in the thing itself; the passionate and predestined Landless, or the half maniacal Jasper carving devils out of his own heart. The workmanship of it is very fine; the right hand has not only not lost, but is still gaining its cunning. But as we turn the now enigmatic pages the thought creeps into us again which I have suggested earlier, and which is never far off the mind of a true lover of Dickens. Had he lost or gained by the growth of technique and probability in his later work? His later characters were more like men; but were not his earlier characters more like immortals? He has become able to perform a social scene so that it is possible at any rate; but where is that Dickens who once performed the impossible? Where is that young poet who created such majors and architects as nature will never dare to create? Dickens learnt to describe daily life as Thackeray and Jane Austen could describe it; but Thackeray could not have thought such a thought as Crummles; and it is painful to think of Miss Austen attempting to imagine Mantalini. After all, we feel there are many able novelists; but there is only one Dickens, and whither has he fled?

He was alive to the end. And in this last dark and secretive story of Edwin Drood he makes one splendid and staggering appearance, like a magician saying farewell to mankind. In the centre of this otherwise reasonable and rather melancholy book, this grey story of a good clergyman and the quiet Cloisterham Towers, Dickens has calmly inserted one entirely delightful and entirely insane passage. I mean the frantic and inconceivable epitaph of Mrs. Sapsea, that which describes her as the "reverential wife" of Thomas Sapsea, speaks of her consistency in "Looking up to him," and ends with the words, spaced out so admirably on the tomb-stone, "Stranger, pause. And ask thyself the question, Canst thou do likewise? If not, with a blush retire." Not the wildest tale in Pickwick contains such an impos-sibility as that; Dickens dare scarcely have introduced it, even as one of Jingle's lies. In no human churchyard will you find that invaluable tombstone; indeed, you could scarcely find it in any world where there are churchyards. You could scarcely have such immortal folly as that in a world where there is also death. Mr. Sapsea is one of the golden things stored up for us in a better world.

Yes, there were many other Dickenses: a clever Dick-ens, an industrious Dickens, a public-spirited Dickens; but this was the great one. This last outbreak of insane humour reminds us wherein lay his power and his su-premacy. The praise of such beatific buffoonery should be the final praise, the ultimate word in his honour. The wild epitaph of Mrs. Sapsea should be the serious epitaph of Dickens.

CHAPTER X

The Great Dickens Characters

ALL criticism tends too much to become criticism of criticism; and the reason is very evident. It is that criticism of creation is so very staggering a thing. We see this in the difficulty of criticizing any artistic creation. We see it again in the difficulty of criticizing that creation which is spelt with a capital C. The pessimists who attack the Universe are always under this disadvantage. They have an exhilarating consciousness that they could make the sun and moon better; but they also have the depressing consciousness that they could not make the sun and moon at all. A man looking at a hippopotamus may sometimes be tempted to regard a hippopotamus as an enormous mistake; but he is also bound to confess that a fortunate inferiority prevents him personally from making such mistakes. It is neither a blasphemy nor an exaggeration to say that we feel something of the same difficulty in judging of the very creative element in human literature. And this is the first and last dignity of Dickens; that he was a creator. He did not point out things, he made them. We may disapprove of Mr. Guppy, but we recognize him as a creation flung down like a miracle out of an upper sphere; we can pull him to pieces, but we could not have put him together. We can destroy Mrs. Gamp in our wrath, but we could not have made her in our joy. Under this disadvantage any book about Dickens must definitely labour. Real primary creation (such as the sun or the birth of a child) calls forth not criticism, not appreciation, but a kind of incoherent gratitude. This is why most hymns about God are bad; and this is why most eulogies on Dickens are bad. The eulogists of the divine and of the human creator are alike inclined to appear sentimentalists because they are talking about something so very real. In the same way love-letters always sound florid and artificial because they are about something real.

Any chapter such as this chapter must therefore in a sense be inadequate. There is no way of dealing properly with the ultimate greatness of Dickens, except by offering sacrifice to him as a god; and this is opposed to the etiquette of our time. But something can perhaps be done in the way of suggesting what was the quality of this creation. But even in considering its quality we ought to remember that quality is not the whole question. One of the godlike things about Dickens is his quantity, his quantity as such, the enormous output, the incredible fecundity of his invention. I have said a moment ago that not one of us could have invented Mr. Guppy. But even if we could have stolen Mr. Guppy from Dickens we have still to confront the fact that Dickens would have been able to invent another quite inconceivable character to take his place. Perhaps we could have created Mr. Guppy; but the effort would certainly have exhausted us; we should be ever afterwards wheeled about in a bath-chair at Bournemouth.

Nevertheless there is something that is worth saying about the quality of Dickens. At the very beginning of this review I remarked that the reader must be in a mood, at least, of democracy. To some it may have sounded irrelevant; but the Revolution was as much behind all the books of the nineteenth century as the Catholic religion (let us say) was behind all the colours and carving of the Middle Ages. Another great name of the nineteenth century will afford an evidence of this; and will also bring us most sharply to the problem of the literary quality of Dickens.

Of all these nineteenth century writers there is none, in the noblest sense, more democratic than Walter Scott. As this may be disputed, and as it is relevant, I will expand the remark. There are two rooted spiritual realities out of which grow all kinds of democratic conception or sentiment of human equality. There are two things in which all men are manifestly unmistakably equal. They are not equally clever or equally muscular or equally fat, as the sages of the modern reaction (with piercing insight) perceive. But this is a spiritual certainty, that all men are tragic. And this, again, is an equally sublime spiritual certainty, that all men are comic. No special and private sorrow can be so dreadful as the fact of having to die. And no freak or deformity can be so funny as the mere fact of having two legs. Every man is important if he loses his life; and every man is funny if he loses his hat, and has to run after it. And the universal test everywhere of whether a thing is popular, of the people, is whether it employs vigorously these extremes of the tragic and the comic. Shelley, for instance, was an aristocrat, if ever there was one in this world. He was a Republican, but he was not a democrat: in his poetry there is every perfect quality except this pungent and popular stab. For the tragic and the comic you must go, say, to Burns, a poor man. And all over the world, the folk literature, the popular literature, is the same. It consists of very dignified sorrow and very undignified fun. Its sad tales are of broken hearts; its happy tales are of broken heads.

These, I say, are two roots of democratic reality. But they have in more civilized literature, a more civilized embodiment or form. In literature such as that of the nineteenth century the two elements appear somewhat thus. Tragedy becomes a profound sense of human dignity. The other and jollier element becomes a delighted sense of human variety. The first supports equality by saying that all men are equally sublime. The second supports equality by observing that all men are equally interesting.

In this democratic aspect the interest and variety of all men, there is, of course, no democrat so great as Dickens. But in the other matter, in the idea of the dignity of all men, I repeat that there is no democrat so great as Scott. This fact, which is the moral and enduring magnificence of Scott, has been astonishingly overlooked. His rich and dramatic effects are gained in almost every case by some grotesque or beggarly figure rising into a human pride and rhetoric. The common man, in the sense of the paltry man, becomes the common man in the sense of the universal man. He declares his humanity. For the meanest of all the modernities has been the notion that the heroic is an oddity or variation, and that the things that unite us are merely flat or foul. The common things are terrible and startling, death, for instance, and first love: the things that are common are the things that are not commonplace. Into such high and central passions the comic Scott character will suddenly rise. Remember the firm and almost stately answer of the preposterous Nicol Jarvie when Helen Macgregor seeks to browbeat him into condoning lawlessness and breaking his bourgeois decency. That speech is a great monument of the middle class. Molière made M. Jourdain talk prose; but Scott made him talk poetry. Think of the rising and rousing voice of the dull and gluttonous Athelstane when he answers and overwhelms De Bracy. Think of the proud appeal of the old beggar in "The Antiquary" when he rebukes the duellists. Scott was fond of describing kings in disguise. But all his characters are kings in disguise. He was, with all his errors, profoundly possessed with the old religious conception (the only possible democratic basis), the idea that man himself is a king in disguise.

In all this Scott, though a Royalist and a Tory, had in the strangest way the heart of the Revolution. For instance, he regarded rhetoric, the art of the orator, as the immediate weapon of the oppressed. All his poor men make grand speeches, as they did in the Jacobin Club, which Scott would have so much detested. And it is odd to reflect that he was, as an author, giving free speech to fictitious rebels while he was, as a stupid politician, denying it to real ones. But the point for us here is this: that all this popular sympathy of his rests on the graver basis, on the dark dignity of man. "Can you find no way?" asks Sir Arthur Wardour of the beggar when they are cut off by the tide. "I'll give you a farm . . . I'll make you rich." . . . "Our riches will soon be equal," says the beggar, and looks out across the advancing sea.

Now, I have dwelt on this strong point of Scott because it is the best illustration of the one weak point of Dickens. Dickens had little or none of this sense of the concealed sublimity of every separate man. Dickens's sense of democracy was entirely of the other kind; it rested on the other of the two supports of which I have spoken. It rested on the sense that all men were wildly interesting and wildly varied. When a Dickens character becomes excited he becomes more and more himself. He does not, like the Scott beggar, turn more and more into man. As he rises he grows more and more into a gargoyle or grotesque. He does not, like the fine speaker in Scott, grow more classical as he grows more passionate, more universal as he grows more intense. The thing can only be illustrated by a special case. Dickens did more than once, of course, make one of his quaint or humble characters assert himself in a serious crisis or defy the powerful. There is, for instance, the quite admirable scene in which Susan Nipper (one of the greatest of Dickens's achievements) faces and rebukes Mr. Dombey. But it is still true (and quite appropriate in its own place and manner) that Susan Nipper remains a purely comic character throughout her speech, and even grows more comic as she goes on. She is more serious than usual in her meaning, but not more serious in her style. Dickens keeps the natural diction of Nipper, but makes her grow more Nipperish as she grows more warm. But Scott keeps the natural diction of Bailie Jarvie, but insensibly sobers and uplifts that style until it reaches a plain and appropriate eloquence. This plain and appropriate eloquence was (except in a few places at the end of "Pickwick") almost unknown to Dickens. Whenever he made comic characters talk sentiment comically, as in the instance of Susan, it was a success, but an avowedly extravagant success. Whenever he made comic characters talk sentiment seriously it was an extravagant failure. Humour was his medium; his only way of approaching emotion. Wherever you do not get humour, you get unconscious humour.

As I have said elsewhere in this book Dickens was deeply and radically English; the most English of our great writers. And there is something very English in this contentment with a grotesque democracy; and in this absence of the eloquence and elevation of Scott.

The English democracy is the most humorous democracy in the world. The Scotch democracy is the most dignified, while the whole abandon and satiric genius of the English populace come from its being quite undignified in every way. A comparison of the two types might be found, for instance, by putting a Scotch Labour leader like Mr. Keir Hardie alongside an English Labour leader like Mr. Will Crooks. Both are good men, honest and responsible and compassionate; but we can feel that the Scotchman carries himself seriously and universally, the Englishman personally and with an obstinate humour. Mr. Hardie wishes to hold up his head as Man, Mr. Crooks wishes to follow his nose as Crooks. Mr. Keir Hardie is very like a poor man in Walter Scott. Mr. Crooks is very like a poor man in Dickens.

Dickens then had this English feeling of a grotesque democracy. By that is more properly meant a vastly varying democracy. The intoxicating variety of men—that was his vision and conception of human brotherhood. And certainly it is a great part of human brotherhood. In one sense things can only be equal if they are entirely different. Thus, for instance, people talk with a quite astonishing gravity about the inequality or equality of the sexes; as if there could possibly be any inequality between a lock and a key. Wherever there is no element of variety, wherever all the items literally have an identical aim, there is at once and of necessity inequality. A woman is only inferior to man in the matter of being not so manly; she is inferior in nothing else. Man is inferior to woman in so far as he is not a woman; there is no other reason. And the same applies in some degree to all genuine differences. It is a great mistake to suppose that love unites and unifies men. Love diversifies them, because love is directed towards individuality. The thing that really unites men and makes them like to each other is hatred. Thus, for instance, the more we love Germany the more pleased we shall be that Germany should be something different from ourselves, should keep her own ritual and conviviality and we ours. But the more we hate Germany the more we shall copy German guns and German fortifications in order to be armed against Germany. The more modern nations detest each other the more meekly they follow each other; for all competition is in its nature only a furious plagiarism. As competition means always similarity, it is equally true that similarity always means inequality. If everything is trying to be green, some things will be greener than others; but there is an immortal and indestructible equality between green and red. Something of the same kind of irrefutable equality exists between the violent and varying creations of such a writer as Dickens. They are all equally ecstatic fulfilments of a separate line of development. It would be hard to say that there could be any comparison or inequality, let us say between Mr. Sapsea and Mr. Elijah Pogram. They are both in the same difficulty; they can neither of them contrive to exist in this world; they are both too big for the gate of birth.

Of the high virtue of this variation I shall speak more adequately in a moment; but certainly this love of mere variation (which I have contrasted with the classicism of Scott) is the only intelligent statement of the common case against the exaggeration of Dickens. This is the meaning, the only sane or endurable meaning, which people have in their minds when they say that Dickens is a mere caricaturist. They do not mean merely that Uncle Pumblechook does not exist. A fictitious character ought not to be a person who exists; he ought to be an entirely new combination, an addition to the creatures already existing on the earth. They do not mean that Uncle Pumblechook could not exist; for on that obviously they can have no knowledge whatever. They do not mean that Uncle Pumblechook's utterances are selected and arranged so as to bring out his essential Pumblechookery; to say that is simply to say that he occurs in a work of art. But what they do really mean is this, and there is an element of truth in it. They mean that Dickens nowhere makes the reader feel that Pumblechook has any kind of fundamental human dignity at all. It is nowhere suggested that Pumblechook will some day die. He is felt rather as one of the idle and evil fairies, who are innocuous and yet malignant, and who live for ever because they never really live at all. This dehumanized vitality, this fantasy, this irresponsibility of creation, does in some sense truly belong to Dickens. It is the lower side of his hilarious human variety. But now we come to the higher side of his human variety, and it is far more difficult to state.

Mr. George Gissing, from the point of view of the passing intellectualism of our day, has made (among his many wise tributes to Dickens) a characteristic complaint about him. He has said that Dickens, with all his undoubted sympathy for the lower classes, never made a working man, a poor man, specifically and highly intellectual. An exception does exist, which he must at least have realized—a wit, a diplomatist, a great philosopher. I mean, of course, Mr. Weller. Broadly, however, the accusation has a truth, though it is a truth that Mr. Gissing did not grasp in its entirety. It is not only true that Dickens seldom made a poor character what we call intellectual; it is also true that he seldom made any character what we call intellectual. Intellectualism was not at all present to his imagination. What was present to his imagination was character—a thing which is not only more important than intellect, but is also much more entertaining. When some English moralists write about the importance of having character, they appear to mean only the importance of having a dull character. But character is brighter than wit, and much more complex than sophistry. The whole superiority of the democracy of Dickens over the democracy of such a man as Gissing lies exactly in the fact that Gissing would have liked to prove that poor men could instruct themselves and could instruct others. It was of final importance to Dickens that poor men could amuse themselves and could amuse him. He troubled little about the mere education of that life; he declared two essential things about it—that it was laughable, and that it was livable. The humble characters of Dickens do not amuse each other with epigrams; they amuse each other with themselves. The present that each man brings in hand is his own incredible personality. In the most sacred sense, and in the most literal sense of the phrase, he "gives himself away." Now, the man who gives himself away does the last act of generosity; he is like a martyr, a lover, or a monk. But he is also almost certainly what we commonly call a fool.

The key of the great characters of Dickens is that they are all great fools. There is the same difference between a great fool and a small fool as there is between a great poet and a small poet. The great fool is a being who is above wisdom rather than below it. That element of greatness of which I spoke at the beginning of this book is nowhere more clearly indicated than in such characters. A man can be entirely great while he is entirely foolish. We see this in the epic heroes, such as Achilles. Nay, a man can be entirely great because he is entirely foolish. We see this in all the great comic characters of all the great comic writers of whom Dickens was the last. Bottom the Weaver is great because he is foolish;

Mr. Toots is great because he is foolish. The thing I mean can be observed, for instance, in innumerable actual characters. Which of us has not known, for instance, a great rustic?—a character so incurably characteristic that he seemed to break through all canons about cleverness or stupidity; we do not know whether he is an enormous idiot or an enormous philosopher; we know only that he is enormous, like a hill. These great, grotesque characters are almost entirely to be found where Dickens found them—among the poorer classes. The gentry only attain this greatness by going slightly mad. But who has not known an unfathomably personal old nurse? Who has not known an abysmal butler? The truth is that our public life consists almost exclusively of small men. Our public men are small because they have to prove that they are in the commonplace interpretation clever, because they have to pass examinations, to learn codes of manners, to imitate a fixed type. It is in private life that we find the great characters. They are too great to get into the public world. It is easier for a camel to pass through the eye of a needle than for a great man to enter into the kingdoms of the earth. The truly great and gorgeous personality, he who talks as no one else could talk and feels with an elementary fire, you will never find this man on any cabinet bench, in any literary circle, at any society dinner. Least of all will you find him in artistic society; he is utterly unknown in Bohemia. He is more than clever, he is amusing. He is more than successful, he is alive. You will find him stranded here and there in all sorts of unknown positions, almost always in unsuccessful positions. You will find him adrift as an impecunious commercial traveller like Micawber. You will find him but one of a batch of silly clerks, like Swiveller. You will find him as an unsuccessful actor, like Crummles. You will find him as an unsuccessful doctor, like Sawyer. But you will always find this rich and reeking personality where Dickens found it—among the poor. For the glory of this world is a very small and priggish affair, and these men are too large to get in line with it. They are too strong to conquer.

It is impossible to do justice to these figures because the essential of them is their multiplicity. The whole point of Dickens is that he not only made them, but made them by myriads; that he stamped his foot, and armies came out of the earth. But let us, for the sake of showing the true Dickens method, take one of them, a very sublime one, Toots. It affords a good example of the real work of Dickens, which was the revealing of a certain grotesque greatness inside an obscure and even unattractive type. It reveals the great paradox of all spiritual things; that the inside is always larger than the outside.

Toots is a type that we all know as well as we know chimney-pots. And of all conceivable human figures he is apparently the most futile and the most dull. He is the blockhead who hangs on at a private school, over-grown and underdeveloped. He is always backward in his lessons, but forward in certain cheap ways of the world; he can smoke before he can spell. Toots is a perfect and pungent picture of the wretched youth. Toots has, as this youth always has, a little money of his own; enough to waste in a semi-dissipation he does not enjoy, and in a gaping regard for sports, in which he could not possibly excel. Toots has, as this youth always has, bits of surreptitious finery, in his case the incomparable ring. In Toots, above all, is exactly rendered the central and most startling contradiction; the contrast between a jauntiness and a certain impudence of the attire, with the profound shame and sheepishness of the visage and

the character. In him, too, is expressed the larger con-
trasts between the external gaiety of such a lad's occu-
pations, and the infinite, disconsolate sadness of his
empty eyes. This is Toots; we know him, we pity him,
and we avoid him. Schoolmasters deal with him in despair or in a heart-breaking patience. His family is vague
about him. His low-class hangers-on (like the Game
Chicken) lead him by the nose. The very parasites that
live on him despise him. But Dickens does not despise
him. Without denying one of the dreary details which
make us avoid the man, Dickens makes him a man
whom we long to meet. He does not gloss over one of
his dismal deficiencies, but he makes them seem suddenly like violent virtues that we would go to the
world's end to see. Without altering one fact he manages to alter the whole atmosphere, the whole universe
of Toots. He makes us not only like, but love; not only
love, but reverence this little dunce and cad. The power
to do this is a power truly and literally to be called
divine.

For this is the very wholesome point. Dickens does
not alter Toots in any vital point. The thing he does
alter is us. He makes us lively where we were bored,
kind where we were cruel, and above all, free for an
universal human laughter where we were cramped in a
small competition about that sad and solemn thing, the
intellect. His enthusiasm fills us, as does the love of God,
with a glorious shame; after all, he has only found in
Toots what we might have found for ourselves. He has
only made us as much interested in Toots as Toots is in
himself. He does not alter the proportions of Toots; he
alters only the scale; we seem as if we were staring at a
rat risen to the stature of an elephant. Hitherto we have
passed him by; now we feel that nothing could induce
us to pass him by; that is the nearest way of putting the

truth. He has not been whitewashed in the least; he has not been depicted as any cleverer than he is. He has been turned from a small fool into a great fool. We know Toots is not clever; but we are not inclined to quarrel with Toots because he is not clever. We are more likely to quarrel with cleverness because it is not Toots. All the examinations he could not pass, all the schools he could not enter, all the temporary tests of brain and culture which surrounded him shall pass, and Toots shall remain like a mountain.

It may be noticed that the great artists always choose great fools rather than great intellectuals to embody humanity. Hamlet does express the æsthetic dreams and the bewilderments of the intellect; but Bottom the Weaver expresses them much better. In the same manner Toots expresses certain permanent dignities in human nature more than any of Dickens's more dignified characters can do it. For instance, Toots expresses admirably the enduring fear, which is the very essence of falling in love. When Toots is invited by Florence to come in, when he longs to come in, but still stays out, he is embodying a sort of insane and perverse humility which is elementary in the lover.

There is an apostolic injunction to suffer fools gladly. We always lay the stress on the word suffer, and interpret the passage as one urging resignation. It might be better, perhaps, to lay the stress upon the word gladly, and make our familiarity with fools a delight, and almost a dissipation. Nor is it necessary that our pleasure in fools (or at least in great and godlike fools) should be merely satiric or cruel. The great fool is he in whom we cannot tell which is the conscious and which the unconscious humour; we laugh with him and laugh at him at the same time. An obvious instance is that of ordinary and happy marriage. A man and a woman cannot live together without having against each other a kind of everlasting joke. Each has discovered that the other is a fool, but a great fool. This largeness, this grossness and gorgeousness of folly is the thing which we all find about those with whom we are in intimate contact; and it is the one enduring basis of affection, and even of respect. When we know an individual named Tomkins, we know that he has succeeded where all others have failed; he has succeeded in being Tomkins. Just so Mr. Toots succeeded; he was defeated in all scholastic examinations, but he was the victor in that visionary battle in which unknown competitors vainly tried to be Toots.

If we are to look for lessons, here at least is the last and deepest lesson of Dickens. It is in our own daily life that we are to look for the portents and the prodigies. This is the truth, not merely of the fixed figures of our life; the wife, the husband, the fool that fills the sky. It is true of the whole stream and substance of our daily experience; every instant we reject a great fool merely because he is foolish. Every day we neglect Tootses and Swivellers, Guppys and Joblings, Simmerys and Flashers. Every day we lose the last sight of Jobling and Chuckster, the Analytical Chemist, or the Marchioness. Every day we are missing a monster whom we might easily love, and an imbecile whom we should certainly admire. This is the real gospel of Dickens; the inexhaustible opportunities offered by the liberty and the variety of man. Compared with this life, all public life, all fame, all wisdom, is by its nature cramped and cold and small. For on that defined and lighted public stage men are of necessity forced to profess one set of accomplishments, to rise to one rigid standard. It is the utterly unknown people, who can grow in all directions like an exuberant tree. It is in our interior lives that we find that people are too much themselves. It is in our private life that we find people intolerably individual, that we find them swelling into the enormous contours, and taking on the colours of caricature. Many of us live publicly with featureless public puppets, images of the small public abstractions. It is when we pass our own private gate, and open our own secret door, that we step into the land of the giants.

CHAPTER XI

On the Alleged Optimism
of Dickens

I<small>N</small> one of the plays of the decadent period, an intellectual expressed the atmosphere of his epoch by referring to Dickens as "a vulgar optimist." I have in a previous chapter suggested something of the real strangeness of such a term. After all, the main matter of astonishment (or rather of admiration) is that optimism should be vulgar. In a world in which physical distress is almost the common lot, we actually complain that happiness is too common. In a world in which the majority is physically miserable we actually complain of the sameness of praise; we are bored with the abundance of approval. When we consider what the conditions of the vulgar really are, it is difficult to imagine a stranger or more splendid tribute to humanity than such a phrase as vulgar optimism. It is as if one spoke of "vulgar martyrdom" or "common crucifixion."

First, however, let it be said frankly that there is a foundation for the charge against Dickens which is implied in the phrase about vulgar optimism. It does not concern itself with Dickens's confidence in the value of existence and the intrinsic victory of virtue; that is not optimism but religion. It is not concerned with his habit of making bright occasions bright, and happy stories happy; that is not optimism, but literature. Nor is it concerned even with his peculiar genius for the description of an almost bloated joviality; that is not optimism, it is simply Dickens. With all these higher variations of optimism I deal elsewhere. But over and above all these there is a real sense in which Dickens laid himself open to the accusation of vulgar optimism, and I desire to put the admission of this first, before the discussion that follows. Dickens did have a disposition to make his characters at all costs happy, or, to speak more strictly, he had a disposition to make them comfortable rather than happy. He had a sort of literary hospitality; he too often treated his characters as if they were his guests. From a host is always expected, and always ought to be expected as long as human civilization is healthy, a strictly physical benevolence, if you will, a kind of coarse benevolence. Food and fire and such things should always be the symbols of the man entertaining men; because they are the things which all men beyond question have in common. But something more than this is needed from the man who is imagining and making men, the artist, the man who is not receiving men, but rather sending them forth.

As I shall remark in a moment in the matter of the Dickens villains, it is not true that he made every one thus at home. But he did do it to a certain wide class of incongruous characters; he did it to all who had been in any way unfortunate. It had indeed its origin (a very beautiful origin) in his realization of how much a little pleasure was to such people. He knew well that the greatest happiness that has been known since Eden is the happiness of the unhappy. So far he is admirable. And as long as he was describing the ecstasy of the poor, the borderland between pain and pleasure, he was at his highest. Nothing that has ever been written about human delights, no Earthly Paradise, no Utopia has ever come so near the quick nerve of happiness as his descriptions of the rare extravagances of the poor; such an admirable description, for instance, as that of Kit Nubbles taking his family to the theatre. For he seizes on the real source of the whole pleasure; a holy fear. Kit tells the waiter to bring the beer. "And the waiter, instead of saying, 'Did you address that language to me?' only said, 'Pot of beer, sir; yes, sir.'" That internal and quivering humility of Kit is the only way to enjoy life or banquets; and the fear of the waiter is the beginning of dining. People in this mood "take their pleasures sadly"; which is the only way of taking them at all.

So far Dickens is supremely right. As long as he was dealing with such penury and such festivity his touch was almost invariably sure. But when he came to more difficult cases, to people who for one reason or another could not be cured with one good dinner, he did develop this other evil, this genuinely vulgar optimism of which I speak. And the mark of it is this: that he gave the characters a comfort that had no especial connection with themselves; he threw comfort at them like alms. There are cases at the end of his stories in which his kindness to his characters is a careless and insolent kindness. He loses his real charity and adopts the charity of the Charity Organization Society; the charity that is not kind, the charity that is puffed up, and that does behave itself unseemly. At the end of some of his stories he deals out his characters a kind of out-door relief.

I will give two instances. The whole meaning of the character of Mr. Micawber is that a man can be always almost rich by constantly expecting riches. The lesson is a really important one in our sweeping modern sociology. We talk of the man whose life is a failure; but

Micawber's life never is a failure, because it is always a crisis. We think constantly of the man who if he looked back would see that his existence was unsuccessful; but Micawber never does look back; he always look forward, because the bailiff is coming to-morrow. You cannot say he is defeated, for his absurd battle never ends; he cannot despair of life, for he is so much occupied in living. All this is of immense importance in the understanding of the poor; it is worth all the slum novelists that ever insulted democracy. But how did it happen, how could it happen, that the man who created this Micawber could pension him off at the end of the story and make him a successful colonial mayor? Micawber never did succeed, never ought to succeed; his kingdom is not of this world. But this is an excellent instance of Dickens's disposition to make his characters grossly and incongruously comfortable. There is another instance in the same book. Dora, the first wife of David Copperfield, is a very genuine and amusing figure; she has certainly far more force of character than Agnes. She represents the infinite and divine in rationality of the human heart. What possessed Dickens to make her such a dehumanized prig as to recommend her husband to marry another woman? One could easily respect a husband who after time and development made such a marriage, but surely not a wife who desired it. If Dora had died hating Agnes we should know that everything was right, and that God would reconcile the irreconcilable. When Dora dies recommending Agnes we know that everything is wrong, at least if hypocrisy and artificiality and moral vulgarity are wrong. There, again, Dickens yields to a mere desire to give comfort. He wishes to pile up pillows round Dora; and he smothers her with them, like Othello.

This is the real vulgar optimism of Dickens; it does exist, and I have deliberately put it first. Let us admit that Dickens's mind was far too much filled with pictures of satisfaction and cosiness and repose. Let us admit that he thought principally of the pleasures of the oppressed classes; let us admit that it hardly cost him any artistic pang to make out human beings as much happier than they are. Let us admit all this, and a curious fact remains.

For it was this too easily contented Dickens, this man with cushions at his back and (it sometimes seems) cotton wool in his ears, it was this happy dreamer, this vulgar optimist who alone of modern writers did really destroy some of the wrongs he hated and bring about some of the reforms he desired. Dickens did help to pull down the debtors' prisons; and if he was too much of an optimist he was quite enough of a destroyer. Dickens did drive Squeers out of his Yorkshire den; and if Dickens was too contented, it was more than Squeers was. Dickens did leave his mark on parochialism, on nursing, on funerals, on public executions, on workhouses, on the Court of Chancery. These things were altered; they are different. It may be that such reforms are not adequate remedies; that is another question altogether. The next sociologists may think these old Radical reforms quite narrow or accidental. But such as they were, the old Radicals got them done; and the new sociologists cannot get anything done at all. And in the practical doing of them Dickens played a solid and quite demonstrable part; that is the plain matter that concerns us here. If Dickens was an optimist he was an uncommonly active and useful kind of optimist. If Dickens was a sentimentalist he was a very practical sentimentalist.

And the reason of this is one that goes deep into Dickens's social reform, and like every other real and desirable thing, involves a kind of mystical contradiction. If we are to save the oppressed, we must have two apparently antagonistic emotions in us at the same time. We must think the oppressed man intensely miserable, and, at the same time, intensely attractive and important. We must insist with violence upon his degradation; we must insist with the same violence upon his dignity. For if we relax by one inch the one assertion, men will say he does not need saving. And if we relax by one inch the other assertion, men will say he is not worth saving. The optimists will say that reform is needless. The pessimists will say that reform is hopeless. We must apply both simultaneously to the same oppressed man; we must say that he is a worm and a god; and we must thus lay ourselves open to the accusation (or the compliment) of transcendentalism. This is, indeed, the strongest argument for the religious conception of life. If the dignity of man is an earthly dignity we shall be tempted to deny his earthly degradation. If it is a heavenly dignity we can admit the earthly degradation with all the candour of Zola. If we are idealists about the other world we can be realists about this world. But that is not here the point. What is quite evident is that if a logical praise of the poor man is pushed too far, and if a logical distress about him is pushed too far, either will involve wreckage to the central paradox of reform. If the poor man is made too admirable he ceases to be pitiable; if the poor man is made too pitiable he becomes merely contemptible. There is a school of smug optimists who will deny that he is a poor man. There is a school of scientific pessimists who will deny that he is a man.

Out of this perennial contradiction arises the fact that there are always two types of the reformer. The first we may call for convenience the pessimistic, the second the optimistic reformer. One dwells upon the fact that souls are being lost; the other dwells upon the fact that they are worth saving. Both, of course, are (so far as that is concerned) quite right, but they naturally tend to a difference of method, and sometimes to a difference of perception. The pessimistic reformer points out the good elements that oppression has destroyed; the optimistic reformer, with an even fiercer joy, points out the good elements that it has not destroyed. It is the case for the first reformer that slavery has made men slavish. It is the case for the second reformer that slavery has not made men slavish. The first describes how bad men are under bad conditions. The second describes how good men are under bad conditions. Of the first class of writers, for instance, is Gorky. Of the second class of writers is Dickens.

But here we must register a real and somewhat startling fact. In the face of all apparent probability, it is certainly true that the optimistic reformer reforms much more completely than the pessimistic reformer. People produce violent changes by being contented, by being far too contented. The man who said that revolutions are not made with rose-water was obviously inexperienced in practical human affairs. Men like Rousseau and Shelley do make revolutions, and do make them with rose-water; that is, with a too rosy and sentimental view of human goodness. Figures that come before and create convulsion and change (for instance, the central figure of the New Testament) always have the air of walking in an unnatural sweetness and calm. They give us their peace ultimately in blood and battle and division; not as the world giveth give they unto us.

Nor is the real reason of the triumph of the too-contented reformer particularly difficult to define. He triumphs because he keeps alive in the human soul an invincible sense of the thing being worth doing, of the war being worth winning, of the people being worth their deliverance. I remember that Mr. William Archer, some time ago, published in his interesting series of interviews, an interview with Mr. Thomas Hardy. That powerful writer was represented as saying, in the course of the conversation, that he did not wish at the particular moment to define his position with regard to the ultimate problem of whether life itself was worth living. There are, he said, hundreds of remediable evils in this world. When we have remedied all these (such was his argument), it will be time enough to ask whether existence itself under its best possible conditions is valuable or desirable. Here we have presented, with a considerable element of what can only be called unconscious humour, the plain reason of the failure of the pessimist as a reformer. Mr. Hardy is asking us, I will not say to buy a pig in a poke; he is asking us to buy a poke on the remote chance of there being a pig in it. When we have for some few frantic centuries tortured ourselves to save mankind, it will then be "time enough" to discuss whether they can possibly be saved. When, in the case of infant mortality, for example, we have exhausted ourselves with the earth-shaking efforts required to save the life of every individual baby, it will then be time enough to consider whether every individual baby would not have been happier dead. We are to remove mountains and bring the millennium, because then we can have a quiet moment to discuss whether the millennium is at all desirable. Here we have the low-water mark of the impotence of the sad reformer. And here we have the reason of the paradoxical triumph of the happy one. His triumph is a religious triumph; it rests upon his perpetual assertion of the value of the human soul and of human daily life. It rests upon his assertion that human life is enjoyable because it is human. And he will never

admit, like so many compassionate pessimists, that
human life ever ceases to be human. He does not merely
pity the lowness of men; he feels an insult to their elevation. Brute pity should be given only to the brutes.
Cruelty to animals is cruelty and a vile thing; but cruelty
to a man is not cruelty, it is treason. Tyranny over a
man is not tyranny, it is rebellion, for man is loyal. Now,
the practical weakness of the vast mass of modern pity
for the poor and the oppressed is precisely that it is
merely pity; the pity is pitiful, but not respectful. Men
feel that the cruelty to the poor is a kind of cruelty to
animals. They never feel that it is injustice to equals;
nay, it is treachery to comrades. This dark, scientific
pity, this brutal pity, has an elemental sincerity of its
own; but it is entirely useless for all ends of social reform. Democracy swept Europe with the sabre when it
was founded upon the Rights of Man. It has done literally nothing at all since it has been founded only upon
the wrongs of man. Or, more strictly speaking, its recent
failures have been due to its not admitting the existence
of any rights or wrongs, or indeed of any humanity.
Evolution (the sinister enemy of revolution) does not
especially deny the existence of God; what it does deny
is the existence of man. And all the despair about the
poor, and the cold and repugnant pity for them, has
been largely due to the vague sense that they have literally relapsed into the state of the lower animals.

A writer sufficiently typical of recent revolutionism—
Gorky—has called one of his books by the eerie and
effective title, "Creatures that Once were Men." That
title explains the whole failure of the Russian revolution. And the reason why the English writers, such as
Dickens, did with all their limitations achieve so many
of the actual things at which they aimed, was that they
could not possibly have put such a title upon a human

book. Dickens really helped the unfortunate in the matters to which he set himself. And the reason is that across
all his books and sketches about the unfortunate might
be written the common title, "Creatures that Still are
Men."

There does exist, then, this strange optimistic reformer; the man whose work begins with approval and
yet ends with earthquake. Jesus Christ was destined to
found a faith which made the rich poorer and the poor
richer; but even when He was going to enrich them, He
began with the phrase, "Blessed are the poor." The
Gissings and the Gorkys say, as an universal literary
motto, "Cursed are the poor." Among a million who
have faintly followed Christ in this divine contradiction,
Dickens stands out especially. He said, in all his reforming utterances, "Cure poverty"; but he said in all his
actual descriptions, "Blessed are the poor." He described
their happiness, and men rushed to remove their sorrow.
He described them as human, and men resented the
insults to their humanity. It is not difficult to see why, as
I said at an earlier stage of this book, Dickens's denunciations have had so much more practical an effect than
the denunciations of such a man as Gissing. Both agreed
that the souls of the people were in a kind of prison.
But Gissing said that the prison was full of dead souls.
Dickens said that the prison was full of living souls.
And the fiery cavalcade of rescuers felt that they had not
come too late.

Of this general fact about Dickens's descriptions of
poverty there will not, I suppose, be any serious dispute. The dispute will only be about the truth of those
descriptions. It is clear that whereas Gissing would say,
"See how their poverty depresses the Smiths or the
Browns," Dickens says, "See how little, after all, their
poverty can depress the Cratchits." No one will deny

that he made a special feature a special study of the subject of the festivity of the poor. We will come to the discussion of the veracity of these scenes in a moment. It is here sufficient to register in conclusion of our examination of the reforming optimist, that Dickens certainly was such an optimist, and that he made it his business to insist upon what happiness there is in the lives of the unhappy. His poor man is always a Mark Tapley, a man the optimism of whose spirit increases if anything with the pessimism of his experience. It can also be registered as a fact equally solid and quite equally demonstrable that this optimistic Dickens did effect great reforms.

The reforms in which Dickens was instrumental were, indeed, from the point of view of our sweeping, social panaceas, special and limited. But perhaps, for that reason especially, they afford a compact and concrete instance of the psychological paradox of which we speak. Dickens did definitely destroy—or at the very least help to destroy—certain institutions; he destroyed those institutions simply by describing them. But the crux and peculiarity of the whole matter is this, that, in a sense, it can really be said that he described these things too optimistically. In a real sense, he described Dotheboys Hall as a better place than it is. In a real sense, he made out the workhouse as a pleasanter place than it can ever be. For the chief glory of Dickens is that he made these places interesting; and the chief infamy of England is that it has made these places dull. Dulness was the one thing that Dickens's genius could never succeed in describing; his vitality was so violent that he could not introduce into his books the genuine impression even of a moment of monotony. If there is anywhere in his novels an instant of silence, we only hear more clearly the hero whispering with the heroine, the villain sharpening his dagger, or the creaking of the machinery that is to give out the god from the machine. He could splendidly describe gloomy places, but he could not describe dreary places. He could describe miserable marriages, but not monotonous marriages. It must have been genuinely entertaining to be married to Mr. Quilp. This sense of a still incessant excitement he spreads over every inch of his story, and over every dark tract of his landscape. His idea of a desolate place is a place where anything can happen; he has no idea of that desolate place where nothing can happen. This is a good thing for his soul, for the place where nothing can happen is hell. But still, it might reasonably be maintained by the modern mind that he is hampered in describing human evil and sorrow by this inability to imagine tedium, this dulness in the matter of dulness. For, after all, it is certainly true that the worst part of the lot of the unfortunate is the fact that they have long spaces in which to review the irrevocability of their doom. It is certainly true that the worst days of the oppressed man are the nine days out of ten in which he is not oppressed. This sense of sickness, and sameness Dickens did certainly fail or refuse to give. When we read such a description as that excellent one—in detail— of Dotheboys Hall, we feel that, while everything else is accurate, the author does, in the words of the excellent Captain Nares in Stevenson's "Wrecker," "draw the dreariness rather mild." The boys at Dotheboys were, perhaps, less bullied, but they were certainly more bored. For, indeed, how could any one be bored with the society of so sumptuous a creature as Mr. Squeers? Who would not put up with a few illogical floggings in order to enjoy the conversation of a man who could say, "She's a rum 'un, is Natur'. . . . Natur' is more easier conceived than described"? The same principle applies to the workhouse in "Oliver Twist." We feel vaguely that neither Oliver nor any one else could be entirely unhappy in the presence of the purple personality of Mr. Bumble. The one thing he did not describe in any of the abuses he denounced was the soul-destroying potency of routine. He made out the bad school, the bad parochial system, the bad debtors' prison as very much jollier and more exciting than they may really have been. In a sense, then, he flattered them; but he destroyed them with the flattery. By making Mrs. Gamp delightful he made her impossible. He gave every one an interest in Mr. Bumble's existence; and by the same act gave every one an interest in his destruction. It would be difficult to find a stronger instance of the utility and energy of the method which we have, for the sake of argument, called the method of the optimistic reformer. As long as low Yorkshire schools were entirely colourless and dreary, they continued quietly tolerated by the public, and quietly intolerable to the victims. So long as Squeers was dull as well as cruel he was permitted; the moment he became amusing as well as cruel he was destroyed. As long as Bumble was merely inhuman he was allowed. When he became human, humanity wiped him out. For in order to do these great acts of justice we must always realize not only the humanity of the oppressed, but even the humanity of the oppressor. The satirist had, in a sense, to create the images in the mind before, as an iconoclast, he could destroy them. Dickens had to make Squeers live before he could make him die.

In connection with the accusation of vulgar optimism, which I have taken as a text for this chapter, there is another somewhat odd thing to notice. Nobody in the world was ever less optimistic than Dickens in his treatment of evil or the evil man. When I say optimistic in this matter I mean optimism, in the modern sense, of an attempt to whitewash evil. Nobody ever made less attempt to whitewash evil than Dickens. Nobody black was ever less white than Dickens's black. He painted his villains and lost characters more black than they really are. He crowds his stories with a kind of villain rare in modern fiction—the villain really without any "redeeming point." There is no redeeming point in Squeers, or in Monck, or in Ralph Nickleby, or in Bill Sikes, or in Quilp, or in Brass, or in Mr. Chester, or in Mr. Pecksniff, or in Jonas Chuzzlewit, or in Carker, or in Uriah Heep, or in Blandois, or in a hundred more. So far as the balance of good and evil in human characters is concerned, Dickens certainly could not be called a vulgar optimist. His emphasis on evil was melodramatic. He might be called a vulgar pessimist.

Some will dismiss this lurid villainy as a detail of his artificial romance. I am not inclined to do so. He inherited, undoubtedly, this unqualified villain as he inherited so many other things, from the whole history of European literature. But he breathed into the blackguard a peculiar and vigorous life of his own. He did not show any tendency to modify his blackguardism in accordance with the increasing considerateness of the age; he did not seem to wish to make his villain less villainous; he did not wish to imitate the analysis of George Eliot, or the reverent scepticism of Thackeray. And all this works back, I think, to a real thing in him, that he wished to have an obstreperous and incalculable enemy. He wished to keep alive the idea of combat, which means, of necessity, a combat against something individual and alive. I do not know whether, in the kindly rationalism of his epoch, he kept any belief in a personal devil in his theology, but he certainly created a personal devil in every one of his books.

A good example of my meaning can be found, for

instance, in such a character as Quilp. Dickens may, for all I know, have had originally some idea of describing Quilp as the bitter and unhappy cripple, a deformity whose mind is stunted along with his body. But if he had such an idea, he soon abandoned it. Quilp is not in the least unhappy. His whole picturesqueness consists in the fact that he has a kind of hellish happiness, an atrocious hilarity that makes him go bounding about like an indiarubber ball. Quilp is not in the least bitter; he has an unaffected gaiety, an expansiveness, an universality. He desires to hurt people in the same hearty way that a good-natured man desires to help them. He likes to poison people with the same kind of clamorous camaraderie with which an honest man likes to stand them drink. Quilp is not in the least stunted in mind; he is not in reality even stunted in body—his body, that is, does not in any way fall short of what he wants it to do. His smallness gives him rather the promptitude of a bird or the precipitance of a bullet. In a word, Quilp is precisely the devil of the Middle Ages; he belongs to that amazingly healthy period when even the lost spirits were hilarious.

This heartiness and vivacity in the villains of Dickens is worthy of note because it is directly connected with his own cheerfulness. This is a truth little understood in our time, but it is a very essential one. If optimism means a general approval, it is certainly true that the more a man becomes an optimist the more he becomes a melancholy man. If he manages to praise everything, his praise will develop an alarming resemblance to a polite boredom. He will say that the marsh is as good as the garden; he will mean that the garden is as dull as the marsh. He may force himself to say that emptiness is good, but he will hardly prevent himself from asking what is the good of such good. This optimism does exist

—this optimism which is more hopeless than pessimism—
this optimism which is the very heart of hell. Against
such an aching vacuum of joyless approval there is only
one antidote—a sudden and pugnacious belief in positive evil. This world can be made beautiful again by
beholding it as a battlefield. When we have defined and
isolated the evil thing, the colours come back into everything else. When evil things have become evil, good
things, in a blazing apocalypse, become good. There are
some men who are dreary because they do not believe
in God; but there are many others who are dreary because they do not believe in the devil. The grass grows
green again when we believe in the devil, the roses grow
red again when we believe in the devil.

No man was more filled with the sense of this belli-
cose basis of all cheerfulness than Dickens. He knew
very well the essential truth, that the true optimist can
only continue an optimist so long as he is discontented.
For the full value of this life can only be got by fighting; the violent take it by storm. And if we have accepted
everything, we have missed something—war. This life of
ours is a very enjoyable fight, but a very miserable truce.
And it appears strange to me that so few critics of
Dickens or of other romantic writers have noticed this
philosophical meaning in the undiluted villain. The
villain is not in the story to be a character; he is there
to be a danger—a ceaseless, ruthless, and uncompromis-
ing menace, like that of wild beasts or the sea. For the
full satisfaction of the sense of combat, which everywhere and always involves a sense of equality, it is necessary to make the evil thing a man; but it is not always
necessary, it is not even always artistic, to make him a
mixed and probable man. In any tale, the tone of which
is at all symbolic, he may quite legitimately be made an
aboriginal and infernal energy. He must be a man only

in the sense that he must have a wit and will to be matched with the wit and will of the man chiefly fighting. The evil may be inhuman, but it must not be impersonal, which is almost exactly the position occupied by Satan in the theological scheme.

But when all is said, as I have remarked before, the chief fountain in Dickens of what I have called cheerfulness, and some prefer to call optimism, is something deeper than a verbal philosophy. It is, after all, an incomparable hunger and pleasure for the vitality and the variety, for the infinite eccentricity of existence. And this word "eccentricity" brings us, perhaps, nearer to the matter than any other. It is, perhaps, the strongest mark of the divinity of man that he talks of this world as "a strange world," though he has seen no other. We feel that all there is is eccentric, though we do not know what is the centre. This sentiment of the grotesqueness of the universe ran through Dickens's brain and body like the mad blood of the elves. He saw all his streets in fantastic perspectives, he saw all his cockney villas as top-heavy and wild, he saw every man's nose twice as big as it was, and every man's eyes like saucers. And this was the basis of his gaiety—the only real basis of any philosophical gaiety. This world is not to be justified as it is justified by the mechanical optimists; it is not be justified as the best of all possible worlds. Its merit is not that it is orderly and explicable; its merit is that it is wild and utterly unexplained. Its merit is precisely that none of us could have conceived such a thing, that we should have rejected the bare idea of it as miracle and unreason. It is the best of all impossible worlds.

CHAPTER XII

A Note on the Future of Dickens

THE hardest thing to remember about our own time, of course, is simply that it is a time; we all instinctively think of it as the Day of Judgment. But all the things in it which belong to it merely as this time will probably be rapidly turned upside down; all the things that can pass will pass. It is not merely true that all old things are already dead; it is also true that all new things are already dead; for the only undying things are the things that are neither new nor old. The more you are up with this year's fashion, the more (in a sense) you are already behind next year's. Consequently, in attempting to decide whether an author will, as it is cantly expressed, live, it is necessary to have very firm convictions about what part, if any part, of man is unchangeable. And it is very hard to have this if you have not a religion; or, at least, a dogmatic philosophy.

The equality of men needs preaching quite as much as regards the ages as regards the classes of men. To feel infinitely superior to a man in the twelfth century is just precisely as snobbish as to feel infinitely superior to a man in the Old Kent Road. There are differences between the man and us, there may be superiorities in us over the man; but our sin in both cases consists in thinking of the small things wherein we differ when we ought to be confounded and intoxicated by the terrible and joyful matters in which we are at one. But here again the difficulty always is that the things near us seem larger than they are, and so seem to be a permanent part of mankind, when they may really be only one of its parting modes of expression. Few people, for instance, realize that a time may easily come when we shall see the great outburst of Science in the nineteenth century as something quite as splendid, brief, unique, and ultimately abandoned, as the outburst of Art at the Renascence. Few people realize that the general habit of fiction, of telling tales in prose, may fade, like the general habit of the ballad, of telling tales in verse, has for the time faded. Few people realize that reading and writing are only arbitrary, and perhaps temporary sciences, like heraldry.

The immortal mind will remain, and by that writers like Dickens will be securely judged. That Dickens will have a high place in permanent literature there is, I imagine, no prig surviving to deny. But though all prediction is in the dark, I would devote this chapter to suggesting that his place in nineteenth century England will not only be high, but altogether the highest. At a certain period of his contemporary fame, an average Englishman would have said that there were at that moment in England about five or six able and equal novelists. He could have made a list, Dickens, Bulwer-Lytton, Thackeray, Charlotte Brontë, George Eliot, perhaps more. Forty years or more have passed and some of them have slipped to a lower place. Some would now say that the highest platform is left to Thackeray and Dickens; some to Dickens, Thackeray, and George Eliot;

some to Dickens, , and Charlotte Brontë. I venture to offer the pro on that when more years have passed a more w lin een effected, Dickens will domir e the wh l ngland nineteenth century; will be left on at platform e.

I ow that this is almost imp nt thing to asse nd tha s tend cy is to bring n dispar- ag g scussins of ot er writers in whic Swin- rn ril ntly emb iled himself in l suggestive udy ckens. But my disparageme of the other ngli ovelists is wl lly relative a ot in the least osit . It is certain t t men will a ays return to such wr r as Thackera with his r emotional autumn, is ing that life a sad acred retrospect, in hi least we s uld fo othing. It is not likely me w ge So, for instance, wise and la me o m time to time return to the lyrists he re enascence, to the delicate poignancy of u Be a they will go back to Thackeray. But I Dickens will bestride and dominate our time as t st figure of Rabelais dominates Du Bellay, dom- inate he Renascence and the world.

Yet e put a negative reason first. The particular things f which Dickens is condemned (and justly con- demned) his critics, are precisely those things which have never evented a man from being immortal. The chief of them the unquestionable fact that he wrote an enormous a ount of bad work. This does lead to a man being put b ow his place in his own time: it does not affect his pe n ment place, to all appearance, at all. Shakespeare, for in ance, and Wordsworth wrote not only an enormous mount of bad work, but an enor- mous amount of eno ously bad work. Humanity edits such writers' works them. Virgil was mistaken in cutting out his inferior : we would have undertaken the job. Moreover in the particular case of Dickens there are special reasons for regarding his bad work as in some sense irrelevant. So much of it was written, as I have previously suggested, under a kind of general ambition that had nothing to do with his special genius; an ambition to be a public provider of everything, a warehouse of all human emotions. He held a kind of literary day of judgment. He distributed bad characters as punishments and good characters as rewards. My meaning can be best conveyed by one instance out of many. The character of the kind old Jew in "Our Mutual Friend" (a needless and unconvincing character) was actually introduced because some Jewish correspondent complains that the bad old Jew in "Oliver Twist" conveyed the suggestion that all Jews were bad. The principle is so lightheadedly absurd that it is hard to imagine any literary man submitting to it for an instant. If ever he invented a bad auctioneer he must immediately balance him with a good auctioneer; if he should have conceived an unkind philanthropist, he must on the spot, with whatever natural agony and toil, imagine a kind philanthropist. The complaint is frank; yet Dickens, who tore people in pieces for much fairer complaints, liked this complaint of his Jewish correspondent. It pleased him to be mistaken for a public arbiter: it pleased him to be asked (in a double sense) to judge Israel. All this is so much another thing, a non-literary vanity, that there is much less difficulty than usual in separating it from his serious genius: and by his serious genius, I need hardly say, I mean his comic genius. Such irrelevant ambitions as this are easily passed over, like the sonnets of great statesmen. We feel that such things can be set aside, as the ignorant experiments of men otherwise great, like the politics of Professor Tyndall or the philosophy of Professor Haeckel. Hence, I think, posterity will not care that Dickens has done bad work, but will know that he has done good.

Again, the other chief accusation against Dickens was that his characters and their actions were exaggerated and impossible. But this only meant that they were exaggerated and impossible as compared with the modern world and with certain writers (like Thackeray or Trollope) who were making a very exact copy of the manners of the modern world. Some people, oddly enough, have suggested that Dickens has suffered or will suffer from the change of manners. Surely this is irrational. It is not the creators of the impossible who will suffer from the process of time: Mr. Bunsby can never be any more impossible than he was when Dickens made him. The writers who will obviously suffer from time will be the careful and realistic writers; the writers who have observed every detail of the fashion of this world which passeth away. It is surely obvious that there is nothing so fragile as a fact, that a fact flies away quicker than a fancy. A fancy will endure for two thousand years. For instance, we all have fancy for an entirely fearless man, a hero: and the Achilles of Homer still remains. But exactly the thing we do not know about Achilles is how far he was possible. The realistic narrators of the time are all forgotten (thank God); so we cannot tell whether Homer slightly exaggerated or wildly exaggerated or did not exaggerate at all, the personal activity of a Mycenæan captain in battle: for the fancy has survived the facts. So the fancy of Podsnap may survive the facts of English commerce: and no one will know whether Podsnap was possible, but only know that he is desirable, like Achilles.

The positive argument for the permanence of Dickens comes back to the thing that can only be stated and cannot be discussed: creation. He made things which nobody else could possibly make. He made Dick Swiveller in a very different sense to that in which Thackeray made Colonel Newcome. Thackeray's creation was observation: Dickens's was poetry, and is therefore permanent. But there is one other test that can be added. The immortal writer, I conceive, is commonly he who does something universal in a special manner. I mean that he does something interesting to all men in a way in which only one man or one land can do. Other men in that land, who do only what other men in other lands are doing as well, tend to have a great reputation in their day and to sink slowly into a second or a third or a fourth place. A parallel from war will make the point clearer. I cannot think that any one will doubt that, although Wellington and Nelson were always bracketed, Nelson will steadily become more important and Wellington less. For the fame of Wellington rests upon the fact that he was a good soldier in the service of England, exactly as twenty similar men were good soldiers in the service of Austria or Prussia or France. But Nelson is the symbol of a special mode of attack, which is at once universal and yet specially English, the sea. Now Dickens is at once as universal as the sea and as English as Nelson. Thackeray and George Eliot and the other great figures of that great England, were comparable to Wellington in this, that the kind of thing they were doing—realism, the acute study of intellectual things—numerous men in France, Germany, and Italy were doing as well or better than they. But Dickens was really doing something universal, yet something that no one but an Englishman could do. This is attested by the fact that he and Byron are the men who, like pinnacles, strike the eye of the Continent. The points would take long to study: yet they may take only a moment to indicate. No one but an Englishman could have filled his books at once with a furious caricature and with a positively furious kind-ness. In more central countries, full of cruel memories of political change, caricature is always inhumane. No one but an Englishman could have described the democracy as consisting of free men, but yet of funny men. In other countries where the democratic issue has been more bitterly fought, it is felt that unless you describe a man as dignified you are describing him as a slave. This is the only final greatness of a man; that he does for all the world what all the world cannot do for itself. Dickens, I believe, did it.

The hour of absinthe is over. We shall not be much further troubled with the little artists who found Dickens too sane for their sorrows and too clean for their delights. But we have a long way to travel before we get back to what Dickens meant: and the passage is along a rambling English road, a twisting road such as Mr. Pickwick travelled. But this at least is part of what he meant; that comradeship and serious joy are not interludes in our travel; but that rather our travels are interludes in comradeship and joy, which through God shall endure for ever. The inn does not point to the road; the road points to the inn. And all roads point at last to an ultimate inn, where we shall meet Dickens and all his characters: and when we drink again it shall be from the great flagons in the tavern at the end of the world.

CHARLES DICKENS: HIS LIFE

By G. K. Chesterton

Reprinted from The Encyclopaedia Britannica

Dickens, Charles John Huffam (1812–1870), certainly the most popular and perhaps the greatest of the great English novelists, was born in Landport, a division of Portsea; in a house in Mile End terrace, Commercial road. The house can be identified and is in some sense a popular shrine or memorial, enabling the sightseer to link up in one journey two of the most romantic national names, associating Dickens with Portsea and Nelson with Portsmouth. But beyond this symbolic and almost legendary local interest, the actual address indicates little more than the drifting and often decaying fortunes of the class and family from which he came. It would be an exaggeration to compare it to Lant street, in the Borough, of which, it will be remembered, "the inhabitants were migratory, disappearing usually towards the verge of quarter-day." But there is the note of something nomadic about the social world to which he belonged. We talk of the solid middle class; he belonged, one might almost say, to the liquid middle class; certainly to the insecure middle class. His father, John Dickens, was a clerk in the Navy Pay-office, and all through life a man of wavering and unstable status, partly by his misfortunes and partly by his fault. It is said that Dickens sketched him in a lighter spirit as Micawber and in a sadder and more realistic aspect as Dorrit. The contrast between the two men, as well as the two moods, should be a warning against the weakness of taking too literally the idea of Dickensian "originals." The habit has done grave injustice to many people, such as Leigh Hunt; and it may involve a grave injustice to John Dickens; and perhaps an even graver injustice to Mrs. John Dickens, née Elizabeth Barrow, whom a similar rumour reports as the real Mrs. Nickleby. Some may question, not without grief, whether there really could be a real Mrs. Nickleby. But in any case there certainly could not be a man who was both Dorrit and Micawber.

214

The truth is that we shall misunderstand from the beginning the nature of the Dickensian imagination, if we suppose these things to be mechanical portraits in black and white, taken by "the profeel machine," as Mr. Weller said. It is the whole point of Dickens that he took hints from human beings; and turned them, one may say, into superhuman beings. But it is true that John Dickens was of the type that is often shifted from place to place; and this is the chief significance of Charles Dickens's connection with Portsea, or rather of his lack of connection with it. He can only have been two years old when the household moved for a short time to London and then for a longer time to Chatham. It was perhaps lucky that the formative period of his first childhood was also the most fortunate period of his not very fortunate family. The dockyard of Chatham, the towers of Rochester, the gardens and the great roads of Kent remained to him through life as the only normal memory of a nursery and a native soil; his house in later years looked down on the great road from Gads-hill and the cathedral tower rose again in his last vision, in the opium dream called "Edwin Drood." Here he had leisure to learn a little from books, who was so soon to learn only from life; first in the stricter sense of school-books, from a Mr. Giles, a Baptist minister in Chatham; and second, and probably with greater profit, from a random heap of old novels that included much of the greatest English literature and even more of the type of literature from which he could learn most; *Roderick Random* and *Robinson Crusoe* and *Tom Jones* and *The Vicar of Wakefield*.

He can hardly have been ten years old when the household was once more upon the march. John Dickens had fallen heavily into debt; he continued the tendency to change his private address; and his next private address was the Debtors' Prison of the Marshalsea. His wife, the mother of eight children of whom Charles was the second, had to encamp desolately in Camden Town and open a dingy sort of "educational establishment." Meanwhile the unfortunate Charles was learning his lessons at a very different sort of educational establishment. After helping his mother in every sort of menial occupation, he was thrown forth to earn his own living by tying and labelling pots of blacking in a blacking warehouse at Old Hungerford Stairs. The blacking was symbolical enough; Dickens never doubted that this piece of his childhood was the darkest period of his life; and he seems indeed to have been in a mood to black himself all over, like the Othello of the Crummles Company. Of his pessimistic period, of the heartrending monotony and ignominy, he has given little more than a bitter abbreviation in *David Copperfield*. But he was storing up much more than bitterness; it is obvious that he had already developed an almost uncanny vigilance and alertness of attention. By the time his servitude came to an end, by his father falling into a legacy as he had fallen into a jail (there was really a touch of Micawber in the way in which things turned up and turned down for him) the boy was no longer a normal boy, let alone a child. He called his wandering parent "the Prodigal Father"; and there was something of the same fantastic family inversion in the very existence of so watchful and critical a son. We are struck at once with an almost malicious maturity of satire; some of the best passages of the prison life of the Pickwicks and the Dorrits occur in private letters about his own early life. He had shared, of course, the improvement in the family condition; which was represented in his case by a period of service as a clerk to a Mr. Blackmore, a Grays Inn solicitor, and afterwards in the equally successful, and much more congenial, occupation of a newspaper reporter and ultimately a Parliamentary reporter. His father had taken up the trade; but his son was already making a mark in it, as reporter to *The True Sun, The Mirror of Parliament* and *The Morning Chronicle*. In all these aspects and attitudes, at this time, he appears as alert, sharp-witted and detached; recalling that sort of metallic brightness which an observer at this period so often saw flash upon his face. It is worthy of note, because certain healthy social emotions which he always championed have somewhat falsified his personality in the eyes of the prigs whom he loved to rap over the head. He was a genuine champion of geniality; but he was not always genial; certainly not only genial. One of his earliest sketches, published not long after this time, was a defence of the Christian festivity of Christmas against the Puritans and the Utilitarians; it was called "Sunday Under Three Heads." All his life he defended valiantly the pleasures of the poor; and insisted that God had given ale and rum, as well as wine, to make glad the heart of man. But all this has clouded his character with fumes of mere conviviality and irresponsibility which were very far from being really characteristic. Even in youth, which is the period of irresponsibility, Dickens appears in some ways as highly responsible. He was in sharp reaction against the futility of his family; he was both ambitious and industrious; and there were some who even found him hard. In many moods he had as angry a dislike of the Skimpoles as of the Gradgrinds.

Indeed he had come in more ways than one to the high turning-point of his fortunes. His marriage and his first real literary work can be dated at about the same time. He had already begun to write sketches, chiefly in the *Old Monthly Magazine,* which were in the broadest sense caricatures, of the common objects of the street or the market-place. They were illustrated by Cruikshank; and in these early stages of the story the illustrator is often more important than the author. This was notoriously true of his next and perhaps his greatest experiment; but it is typical in any case of his time and his time of life. The prose sketches were signed "Boz" and the signature had become a recognized pseudonym when Messrs. Chapman and Hall, the publishers, approached him with the suggestion of a larger scheme. A well-known humorous artist of that epoch, Seymour, was to produce a series of plates illustrating the adventures, or misadventures, of the Nimrod Club, a group of amateur sportsmen, destined to dwindle and yet to grow infinitely greater in the single figure of Mr. Nathaniel Winkle. Dickens consented to write the letterpress, which was little more than a running accompaniment like an ornamental border around the drawings; and in that strange fashion, secondary, subordinate and even trivial, first formed itself in the human fancy the epic and pantomime of *Pickwick* (1837). Dickens persuaded the publishers to let the Pickwick Club represent more varied interests or eccentricities, retained Mr. Winkle to represent or misrepresent the original notion of sport; and by that one stroke of independence cut himself free from a stale fashion and started a new artistic adventure and revolution. He gave as one of his reasons the fact that he had no special knowledge of sports or games, and proceeded to drive his argument home triumphantly by his description of the cricket-match at Dingley Dell. And yet that cricket-match alone might illustrate exactly the game which Dickens so gloriously won; and why that wild and ill-instructed batsman has had so many thousand runs and is not out. What did a few mistakes in the description of cricket, or even in the description of real life, matter in a man who could invent that orator at the cricket-dinner, who complimented the defeated eleven by saying, with the gesture of Alexander, "If I were not Dumkins, I would be Luffey; if I were not Podder, I would be Struggles"? Men do not read that sort of thing to learn about cricket, or even about life, but to find something more living than either. There had broken through the entanglements of that trumpery bargain a force of comic genius which swallowed up its own origin and excuses; a wild animal big enough to eat all its direction labels. People forgot about Seymour; forgot about sport; forgot about the Nimrod Club; soon forgot about the Pickwick Club. They forgot all that he forgot and followed whatever he followed; much bigger and wilder game than any aimed at by the mere gun of Mr. Winkle. The track of the story wandered; the tone of the story changed; a servant whom Pickwick found cleaning boots in an inn-yard took the centre of the stage and towered even over Pickwick; Pickwick from being a pompous buffoon became a generous and venerable old English gentleman; and the world still followed that incredible transformation-scene and wishes there were more of it to this day. This was the emergence of Dickens into literature. It had, of course, many secondary effects in life. One was the first and almost the most bitter of his quarrels; Seymour may be excused for having been annoyed at the relations of artist and author being thus turned upside down in a whirlwind; but Seymour was not therefore necessarily justified in saying, as he did say and his widow long continued to say, that Dickens had gained glory from another man's ideas. Nobody, we may well imagine, believes that the oration of Serjeant Buzfuz or the poem of Mrs. Leo Hunter, were Mr. Seymour's ideas. Dickens had an inexhaustible torrent of such ideas; and no man on earth could pretend to have provided them. But it is true that in this quarrel, as in others, some found a touch of sharpness and acid self-defence in Dickens; and he was never without his enemies. His ideal was certainly the leisure and geniality of Pickwick; but he was fighting rather too hard for his own hand and had too much at stake and too pressing a knowledge of poverty to be anything but practical.

As Pickwick was the foundation of his public life, his marriage was naturally the foundation of his private life; and in this also he has been an object of criticism as he was certainly an object of sympathy. Very little good is done by making guesses about a story of which the spiritual balance and proportion were probably never known to more than three or four people. It is sufficiently significant that those who were nearest to it, and who survive to speak or rather to be silent, agree in laying no very heavy blame upon anyone involved. One of the principals of the *Morning Chronicle,* George Hogarth, had been so much struck by the "Boz" sketches as to insist on an improvement in the payment of the writer; he introduced Dickens to his family and especially (we may say) to his daughters, with all of whom the young journalist seems to have been on very friendly and even affectionate terms. One of them, Catherine, he married, and certainly married for love; but not perhaps with the sort of love which gives a man a full and serious realization of what he is doing. It is the pathos of the story that in a sense the friendship outlasted the love; for another sister, who understood him better, remained his friend long after his marriage had become a prolonged misunderstanding. All this, however, happened long afterwards; for a moment his marriage may be taken as marking his step into security and success; especially as he was probably stimulated and, as it were, intoxicated, by a romance that brought him into more refined social surroundings than his own. From that moment he was launched as a popular writer and a power in the world; and he never went back, until he died of popularity thirty years afterwards.

It is notable that his next work was *Oliver Twist* (1838); which might be meant for a contrast to *Pickwick*. If the first trick had succeeded, nobody could accuse the conjurer of trying the same trick twice. He was probably proud of proving his range; but he was certainly courageous in testing his popularity. It is true that *Oliver Twist* consists of a queer mixture of melodrama and realism; but both the realism and the melodrama are deliberately dark and grim. Nevertheless it is fortunate that with his second book he thus brought into play what may be called his second talent. It is too common to compare his humour with his pathos; for indeed there is no comparison. But there really is a comparison between his humour and his horror; and he really had a talent for a certain sort of horror, which is exactly rendered by the popular phrase of supping on horrors. For there is a sort of lurid conviviality that accompanies the panic; as if the nightmare could accompany and not follow the heavy meal. This suppressed vitality is due to his never for an instant losing the love of life; the love of death, which is despair and pessimism, was meaningless to him till he died. The sort of horror which afterwards conceived the death of Krook is already found in *Oliver Twist*; as in that intolerable repetition throbbing in the murderer's ears; "will wash out mud-stains, blood-stains" and so on. For the rest, the plot is preposterous and the flashes of fun excellent but few; yet there is another aspect of the book which makes it important in the story of Dickens. It is not only the first of his nightmare novels, but also the first of his social tracts. Something of social protest could be read between the lines of Pickwick in prison; but the prison of Pickwick was very mild compared with the charitable almshouse of Oliver. Dickens is witness, with Hood and Cobbett and many others, that the workhouse was felt by all generous people as something quite unnaturally new and hard and inhuman. It is sometimes said that he killed Bumble; it would be truer to say that, by making Bumble live, he created something by which it will always be possible to kill bureaucracies.

Whether we call the transition from *Pickwick* to *Oliver Twist* a change from comedy to tragedy, or merely a change from farce to melodrama, it is notable that the next act of Dickens is to mix the two in about equal proportions. Having shown how much he can vary, he tries to show how well he can combine. It is worth noting because it explains much of the failure as well as the success of his art as a whole. We may even say that, to the last, this sort of exhibition of power remained his principal weakness. When the critics, like those of *The Quarterly,* called him vulgar, it meant nothing except that the critics themselves were snobbish. There is nothing vulgar about drinking beer or describing the drinking of beer, or enjoying the humours of really humorous people who happen to black boots, like Sam Weller. But there is something just a little vulgar about professing to be a Universal Provider; a man who writes not only something that he wants to write, but anything that anybody wants to read. Anything in his work that can really be called failure is very largely due to this appetite for universal success. There is nothing wrong about the jester laughing at his own jokes; indeed they must be very poor jokes if even he cannot laugh at them. Dickens, in one of those endless private letters which are almost more entertaining than his published novels, describes himself as "a gentleman with rather long hair and no neck.

cloth, who writes and grins, as if he thought he was very funny indeed"; and so he was. But when he set out to prove that he was not only very funny, but very pathetic, very tragic, very powerful, he was not always enjoying the sense of power over his work, he was enjoying the sense of power over his audience. He was an admirable actor in private theatricals; and sometimes, unfortunately, they were public theatricals. And on this side of his character he had the proverbial itch of Toole to act Hamlet. When he was rendering the humours of the crowd, he was that rather rare thing, a real democrat. But when he was trying to command the tears and thrills of the crowd, he was something of a demagogue; that is, not one mingling with the crowd, but one trying to dazzle and to drive it. One of the ways in which he displayed this attribute, if not of vulgarity at least of vanity, was in his habit, from this time onwards, of running side by side in the same book about five different stories in about five different styles. It pleased the actor in him to show his versatility and his ease in turning from one to the other. He did not realize clearly enough that in some of the parts he was a first-rate actor and in some a second-rate and in some a fifth-rate actor. He did not remind himself that though he turned to each topic with equal ease, he did not turn to each with equal effect. But, whatever the disadvantages of the universal ambition, it definitely dates from the period of his next book. *Pickwick* has a prevailing tint of gaiety and *Oliver Twist* of gravity, not to say grimness; but with *Nicholas Nickleby* (1839) we have the new method, which is like a pattern of bright and dark stripes. The melodrama is if possible even more melodramatic than in *Oliver Twist;* but what there is of it is equally black and scowling. But the comedy or farce has already displayed the rapid ripening of his real genius in letters. There is no better company in all literature than the strolling company of Mr. Vincent Crummles; though it is to be hoped that in any convivial meeting of it, Miss Snevellicci will remember to invite her incomparable papa. Mr. Mantalini also is one of the great gifts of Dickens to the enduring happiness of humanity. For the rest, it is very difficult to take the serious part of the story seriously. There is a precious little difference between the rant and claptrap of the Crummles plays, which Dickens makes fun of, and the rant and claptrap of Ralph Nickleby and Mulberry Hawk which Dickens gravely narrates to us. All that, however, was of little consequence either immediate or permanent. Dickens was not proving that he could write smooth and probable narratives, which many people could do. He was proving that he could create Mantalini and Snevellicci, which nobody could do.

Nevertheless, this pretence of providing for all tastes, which produced the serio-comic novel, is also the explanation of the next stage of his career. There runs or recurs throughout his whole life a certain ambition to preside over a more or less complex or many-sided publication; a large framework for many pictures; a system of tales within tales like the Arabian Nights or the tales of the Tabard. It is the ambition that he afterwards gratified by becoming the editor of two magazines, *Household Words* and *All the Year Round*. But there is here something of a shadow of the original meaning of the word magazine, in the sense of a shop; and another hint of that excessive desire to keep a shop that sells everything. He had been for a time editor of something of the sort in *Bentley's Miscellany*, but the final form taken by this mild and genial megalomania (if we may so describe it) was the plan which Dickens formed immediately after the success of *Nicholas Nickleby*. The serial scheme was to be called, "Master Humphrey's Clock," and was to consist of different stories told by a group of friends. With the idea of making them the more friendly he turned some of them into old friends; reintroducing Mr. Pickwick and the two Wellers, though these characters were hardly at their best, the author's mind being already on other things. One of these things was a historical novel, perhaps conceived more in the romantic manner of Scott than the prosaic manner of Smollett, which Dickens generally followed. It was called *Barnaby Rudge* (1840) and the most interesting part of it perhaps is the business of the Gordon Riots; and the mob that has a madman for its mascot and a penny-dreadful prentice for its comic relief. But there is also a plot as complicated as, though rather clearer than, that of *Oliver Twist;* a plot that intensely interested the detective mind of Poe. *Barnaby Rudge,* however, is not so directly Dickensian as the romance that preceded or the romance that followed it. The second story, somewhat insecurely wedged into the framework of *Master Humphrey's Clock,* was *The Old Curiosity Shop* (1841), as the opening and some of the references in the story still vaguely attest. The public reception of this story very sharply illustrates what has been said about the double character of his success. On the one side was his true success as a craftsman carving figures of a certain type, generally gargoyles and grotesques. On the other side was his inferior success as a jack-of-all-trades tending only too much to be a cheap-jack. As a matter of fact, *The Old Curiosity Shop* contains some of the most attractive and imaginative humour in all his humorous work; there is nothing better anywhere than Mr. Swiveller's imitation of the brigand or Mr. Brass's funeral oration over the dwarf. But in general gossip and association, everything else in the story is swallowed up in the lachrymose subject of Little Nell. There can be no doubt that this unfortunate female had a most unfortunate effect on Dickens's whole conception of his literary function. He was flattered because silly people wrote him letters imploring him not to let Little Nell die; and forgot how many sensible people there were, only hoping that the Marchioness would live for ever. Little Nell was better dead, but she was an unconscionable long time dying; and we cannot altogether acquit Dickens of keeping her lingering in agony as an exhibition of his power. It tended to fix him in that unfortunate attitude, of something between a showman and a magician, which explains almost all the real mistakes of his life.

About this time a very determining event interrupted his purely literary development, his first visit to America. It was destined to have, apart from any other results, a direct effect upon his next book, which was *Martin Chuzzlewit* (1844). There were, of course, many purely practical and personal elements in the criticism which he directed against the western democracy. An unjust copyright law, or one which he at any rate thought very unjust, had enabled Americans to pirate his most popular works; and it would seem that the people he met were, in their breezy way, but little inclined to apologize for the anomaly. But it would be very unjust to Dickens to deny that his sense and sensibility were alike irritated by some real divisions in the international relation. There were things in the American culture, or lack of culture, which he could not be expected to understand but which he might reasonably be expected to dislike. His English law-abiding liberalism would in any case have been startled by a certain streak of ferocity and persecution that there really is in the Americans; just as he might have recoiled from the same fierceness in the Irish or the Italians. But in the Americans it was also connected with something crude and incomplete in the society, and was not softened by tradition or romance. He was also both annoyed and amused at the American habit of uttering solemn idealistic soliloquies and of using rhetoric very rhetorically. But all these impressions are important chiefly as they changed the course of his next important narrative; and illustrated a certain condition or defect of his whole narrative method.

All these early books of Dickens, from *Pickwick* onward, appeared, it must always be remembered, serially and in separate parts. They were anticipated eagerly like bulletins; and they were often written up to time almost as hastily as newspaper reports. One effect of this method was that it encouraged the novelist in a sort of opportunism and something of a hand-to-mouth habit of work. And a character that always belonged, in varying degrees, to his novels is first and most sharply illustrated in *Martin Chuzzlewit*. The earlier numbers, though they contained the two superb caricatures called Pecksniff and Mrs. Gamp, had not for some reason been so popular as the caricatures called Pick-wick and Miss Squeers. Dickens was already beginning to show something of that feverish fatigue which was the nat-ural reaction of his fervid industry. He feared that the pub-lic was bored with the book; he became perhaps subcon-sciously a little bored with it himself. He conceived the bold idea of breaking the story in the middle and putting in a purple patch woven from his wild memories of the Yankees. It was completely successful, in the comedy sense; but it is worth noting that Dickens did something curiously Dickensian in thus suddenly sending Martin Chuzzlewit across the sea to America. It is not easy to imagine Thack-eray suddenly hurling Pendennis from Mayfair into the middle of Australia; or George Eliot dislodging Felix Holt and flinging him as far as the North Pole. The difference was partly the result of the Dickensian temper and partly of the method of publication. But it will be well to remem-ber it: for there is more than one example of what looks like a positive change of plan in the Dickens stories, made more possible by this early habit of not producing the work of art as a whole. Some have suggested that the degenera-tion of Boffin was originally meant to be real, and his rather clumsy plot an afterthought: and the same idea has figured in the reconstructions of *Edwin Drood*.

At this point there is a break in the life of Dickens, in more ways than one. It is represented by his decision to live abroad for a time, chiefly on grounds of economy; the last lingering results of the relative failure of *Martin Chuzzle-wit*. He took a villa in the neighbourhood of Genoa in 1844; and he and his family, already a fairly large one, settled down there with a certain air of finality that de-served for a time the name of exile. But it is curious to note that the literary work done there has something of the char-acter of an interlude, and indeed of a rather incongruous interlude. For it was in that Italian landscape that he con-centrated on a study so very domestic, insular and even cockney as *The Chimes* (1845); and industriously continued the series of short Christmas stories which had recently begun in the very London fog of *A Christmas Carol* (1843). Whatever be the merits or demerits of *A Christmas Carol,* it really is a carol; in the sense of being short and direct and having the same chorus throughout. The same is true in another way of *The Chimes;* and of most things that occupied him in his Italian home. He had not settled down to another long and important book; and it soon became apparent that he had not settled down at all. He returned to London, the landscape which for him was really the most romantic and even historic; and did something so ominously typical of the place and time as almost to seem like tempting Providence. He became the first editor of *The Daily News,* a paper started to maintain those Liberal, if not Radical opinions of which he always shared the confident outlook and the humane simplicity. He did not long remain attached to the editorial chair or even to the metropolis, for this was the most restless period in all his restless life. He immediately went back to Lausanne and immediately wanted to go back to London. It seems probable that this break in his social life corresponded to a break in his artistic life: which was in a sense just about to begin all over again and begin at the other end. He did indeed write one more full-size novel of the earlier type, *Dombey and Son* (1846–48); but it has very much the character of the winding up of an old business, like the winding up of the Dombey firm at the end of it. It is comic as the earlier books were comic, and no praise can be higher; it is conventional as the earlier plots were conventional, and never really pretended to be anything else; it contains a dying child upon the pattern of Little Nell; it contains a very amusing major much improved from the pattern of Mr. Dowler. But underneath all this easy repetition of the old dexterity and the old clumsiness the mind of the conjurer is already elsewhere. *Dombey and Son* was more successful in a business sense than *Martin Chuzzlewit;* though really less successful in many others. Dickens settled again in England in a more prosperous style; sent his son to Eton and, what was more sensational, took a rest. It was after a long holiday at Broadstairs, in easier circumstances more favourable to imaginative growth and a general change of view, that there appeared in 1849 an entirely new novel in an entirely new style.

There is all the difference between the life and adventures of David Copperfield and the life and adventures of Nicholas Nickleby, that there is between the life of Charles Dickens and the life of Amadis of Gaul. The latter is a good or bad romance; the former is a romantic biography, only the more realistic for being romantic. For romance is a very real part of life and perhaps the most real part of youth. Dickens had turned the telescope round or was looking through the other end of it; looking perhaps into a mirror, looking in any case out of a new window. It was life as he saw it, which was somewhat fantastically; but it was his own life as he knew it, and even as he had lived it. In other words, it is fanciful but it is not fictitious; because not merely invented in the manner of fiction. In Pickwick or Nickleby he had in a sense breathed fresh imaginative life into stock characters, but they were still stage characters; in the new style he may be extravagant, but he is not stagey. That vague glow of exaggeration and glamour which lies over all the opening chapters of *David Copperfield*, which dilates some figures and distorts others, is the genuine sentimentalism and suppressed passion of youth; it is no longer a convention or tradition of caricature. There are men like Steerforth and girls like Dora; they are not as boys see them; but boys do see them so. This passionate autobiography, though it stiffens into greater conventionality at the real period of passion, is really, in the dismally battered phrase, a human document. But something of the new spirit, more subtle and sympathetic but perhaps less purely creative, belongs to all the books written after this date. The next of the novels in point of time was *Bleak House* (1853), a satire chiefly directed against Chancery and the law's delay, but containing some brilliant satire on other things, as on the philanthropic fool whose eyes are in the ends of the earth. But the description of the feverish idleness of Rick has the new note of one for whom a well-meaning young man is no longer merely a "first walking gentleman." After a still more severe phase in *Hard Times* (1854) (historically important as the revolt of a Radical against the economic individualism which was originally identified with Radicalism) he continued the same tendency in *Little Dorrit* (1857), the tone of which is perhaps as sad as anything illustrated by Dickensian humours can be; broke off into an equally serious and more sensational experiment in historical romance in *A Tale of Two Cities* (1859), largely an effect of the influence of Carlyle; and finally reached what was perhaps the height of his new artistic method in a purely artistic sense. He never wrote anything better, considered as literature, than the first chapters of *Great Expectations* (1861). But there is, after all, something about Dickens that prevents the critic from being ever quite content with criticizing his work as literature. Something larger seems involved, which is not literature, but life; and yet the very opposite of a mere recorded way of living. And he who remembers Pickwick and Pecksniff, creatures like Puck or Pan, may sometimes wonder whether the work had not most life when it was least lifelike.

The stretch of stories following on *David Copperfield,* from 1850 onwards, fall into the framework of another of Dickens's editorial schemes; and this time a much more successful one. He began to edit *Household Words,* in which some, though not all of his later tales appeared; and continued to do so until he exchanged it in 1859 for another and similar periodical called *All the Year Round.* Just as we find him about this time induced at last to settle down finally in a comparatively comfortable editorial chair, so we find him at last settled more comfortably in a domicile that could really be called a home, when, returning at last to his beloved Rochester district on the great road of Kent, he set up his house at Gads-hill. It is sad to realize that this material domestic settlement had followed on a moral unsettlement; and the separation of Dickens and his wife, by agreement (of which the little that needs saying has already been said) had already taken place in 1856. But indeed, even apart from that tragedy, it is typical of Dickens that his repose could never be taken as final. His life was destined to end in a whirlwind of an entirely new type of activity; which none the less never interrupted that creative work which was the indwelling excitement of all his days. He wrote one more complete novel, *Our Mutual Friend* (1864–65), and it is more complete than most. Indeed it is one of the best though not one of the most Dickensian of the Dickens novels. He then turned his restless talent to something in the nature of a detective story, more in the manner of his friend Wilkie Collins; the sort of story which begins by asking a question; in this case a question about the secret and the sequel of the fate of the hero, Edwin Drood. The question will never be answered; for it was cut short by the only thing that could be more dramatic than the death of the hero; the death of the author. Charles Dickens was dead.

He died very suddenly, dropping from his chair at the dinner-table, in the year 1870 at the comparatively early age of fifty-eight. A death so abrupt, and essentially so premature, could not but raise doubts about the wisdom of his impetuous industry and debates almost as varied as those round the secret of Edwin Drood. But without exaggerating any one of the elements that contributed to it, we may note that the very last phase of his life was a new phase; and was almost entirely filled with his new activity in giving public readings from his works. He had gone to America once more in the November of 1867, with this particular purpose; and his campaign of public speaking in this style was truly American in its scope and scale. If he had indeed been unjust to America as a writer, it is curious that he should have reached his final popularity and perhaps his final collapse, in a character so supremely American. Differences exist about how far he exaggerated the function or how far his biographer exaggerated the danger; but his own letters, ragged with insomnia and impatience, full of desperate fatigue and more desperate courage, are alone enough to show that he was playing a very dangerous game for a man approaching sixty. But it is certainly true, as is alleged on the other side, that this was nothing new in the general conduct of Dickens; that he had long ago begun burning the candle at both ends; and there have been few men, in the matter of natural endowments, with so great and glorious a candle to burn.

He was buried in the Poets' Corner of Westminster Abbey; and new and vulgar as many critics had called his work, he was far more of a poet than many who were buried there as poets. He left a will commending his soul to God, and to the mercy of Jesus Christ, and leaving his works to the judgment of posterity; and in both respects the action was symbolic and will remain significant in history. Intellectually limited as he was by the rather cheap and cheery negations of an age of commercial rationalism, he had never been a bitter secularist or anti-clerical; he was at heart traditional and was drawn much more towards Anglican than Puritan Christianity; and his greatest work may yet prove to be the perpetuation of the joyful mystery of Christmas. On the other side, he has suffered and may suffer again the changes in the mere fashions of criticism; but his work was creative, it added something to life; and it is hard to believe that something so added will ever be entirely taken away. The defects of his work are glaring; they hardly need to be detected; they need the less to be emphasized because, unfortunately, he always emphasized them himself. It may be a fault, it is certainly a fact, that he enjoyed writing his worst work as much as his best.

The charge of exaggeration is itself exaggerated. It is also, which is much more important, merely repeated mechanically, without any consideration of its true meaning. Dickens did exaggerate; but his exaggeration was purely Dickensian. In this sense his very vulgarity had the quality of distinction. Mere overstatement, to say that a tall man is ten feet high, to say that a frosty morning froze Niagara; this is something relatively easy to do, though sometimes very cleverly done, especially by Americans. But the distinction of Dickens can be stated even in the common charge against him. He is said to have turned men into monsters of humour or horror, whereas the men were really commonplace and conventional persons in shops and offices. If any critic depreciates the Dickensian method as mere overstatement, the answer is obvious: let him take some of these commonplace people and overstate them. He will soon discover that he has not the vaguest notion of what to overstate. He will soon realize that it is not a simple matter of mere exaggeration, in the sense of mere extension. It is not a matter of making a man a little taller or a morning a little colder; the challenge to imagination is not whether he can exaggerate, but whether he can find anything worth exaggerating. Now the genius of Dickens consisted in seeing in somebody, whom others might call merely prosaic, the germ of a sort of prose poem. There was in this or that man's attitude, or affectation, or habit of thought, something which only needed a touch of exaggeration to be a charming fantasy or a dramatic contradiction. The books of Dickens are in fact full of bores; of bores who do not bore us, merely because they did not bore him. We have all of us heard a hundred times the tiresome trick of public speakers, of asking themselves rhetorical questions which they do not want answered. Any of us might have heard a fat Dissenting minister doing it at a tea-party and thankfully forgotten all about him. But Dickens seized on the fallacy and turned it into a fantasy; into Mr. Chadband's demands to know why he could not fly, or his wild and beautiful apologue about the elephant and the eel. We talk of the power of drawing people out; and that is the nearest parallel to the power of Dickens. He drew reels and reels of highly coloured caricature out of an ordinary person, as dazzlingly as a conjurer draws reels and reels of highly coloured paper out of an ordinary hat. But if anybody thinks the conjuring-trick is easy to perform, let him try it with the next ordinary person he sees. The exaggeration is always the logical extension of something that really exists; but genius appears, first in seeing that it exists, and second in seeing that it will bear to be thus exaggerated. That is something totally different from giving a man a long nose; it is the delicate surgical separation or extension of a living nerve. It is carrying a ludicrous train of thought further than the actual thinker carries it; but it requires a little thinking. It is making fools more gloriously foolish than they can be in this vale of tears; and it is not every fool who can do it.

There were other reasons for the injustice in the particular case of Dickens. Though his characters often were caricatures, they were not such wild caricatures as was supposed by those who had never met such characters. And the critics had never met the characters; because the critics did not live in the common life of the English people; and Dickens did. England was a much more amusing and horrible place than it appeared to the sort of man who wrote reviews in *The Quarterly;* and, in spite of all scientific progress or social reform, it is still. The poverty and anarchy of Dickens's early life had stuffed his memory with strange things and people never to be discovered in Tennysonian country houses or even Thackerayan drawing-rooms. Poverty makes strange bedfellows, the same sort of bedfellows whom Mr. Pickwick fought for the recovery of his nightcap. In the vivid phrase, he did indeed live in Queer street and was acquainted with very queer fish. And it is something of an irony that his tragedy was the justification of his farce. He not only learnt in suffering what he taught in song, but what he rendered, so to speak, in a comic song.

It is also true, however, that he caught many of these queer fish because he liked fishing in such troubled waters. A good example of this combination of opportunity and eccentricity is to be found in his affection for travelling showmen and vagabond entertainments of all sorts, especially those that exhibited giants and dwarfs and such monstrosities. Some might see in this truth a sort of travesty of all his travesties. It would be easy to suggest a psychological theory, by which all his art tended to the antics of the abnormal; it would also be entirely false. It would be much truer to say that Dickens created so many wild and fantastic caricatures because he was himself commonplace. He never identifies himself with anything abnormal, in the more modern manner. In his travelling show, the Giant always falls far short of being a Superman. And though he was tempted only too easily to an obvious pathos, there was never anything particularly pathetic about his dwarfs. His fun is more robust; and even, in that sense, more callous. The truth is that Dickens's attitude to the abnormal has been misunderstood owing to the modern misunderstanding of the idea of the normal. He was in many ways a wild satirist, but still a satirist; and satire is founded on sanity. He had his real cockney limitations. But his moderation was not a limitation but a liberty; for it allowed him to hit out in all directions. It was precisely because he had an ordinary and sensible view of life that he could measure the full madness both of Gradgrind's greed or Micawber's improvidence. It was because he was what we call commonplace that Dombey appeared to him so stiff or Jellaby so slovenly. In a later generation a real person often assumed such an unreal pose and lost the power of merely laughing at it; as, for example, when Oscar Wilde said seriously all that Skimpole had said absurdly. The Victorian common sense was not a complete common sense; and Dickens did suffer from having a narrower culture than Swift or Rabelais. But he did not suffer from being sensible; it was even more from his sense than his sensibility, it was from a sort of inspired irritation and impatience of good sense, that he was able to give us so radiant a fairyland of fools.

His literary work produced of course much more than a literary effect. He was the last great poet, in the true sense of maker, who made something for the people and was in the highest sense popular. He still gives his name, not to a literary clique, but to a league or fellowship numbering thousands all over the world. In this connection it is often noted that he achieved many things even considered as a practical political and social reformer. He let light into dark corners, like the dens of dirt and brutality often called schools, especially in Yorkshire; he probably had much to do with making the professional nurse a duller but more reliable person than Mrs. Gamp; it is likely enough that his vivid descriptions, assisted by the whole trend of the time, hastened the extinction of ordinary imprisonment for debt and clarified much of the original chaos of Chancery. But precisely because this has often been said, it will be well not to say it too often. It has the effect of making his satire appear much more superficial and utilitarian than it really was; for the great satirist is concerned with things not so easily destroyed. We do more honour to Dickens in noting the evils he did not destroy than those he did. The eager worship of a man merely wealthy, however dull and trivial, which appears in the affair of Merdle, has by no means disappeared from our own more recent affairs. The pompous old Barnacle and the agreeable young Barnacle are still almost as much alive as in Dickens's day. The sweeping away of a genuine gentry, in the person of Mr. Twemlow, on the tide of a new plutocracy, represented by Mr. Veneering, has gone much further than in Dickens's day. But this makes Dickens's satire the more rather than the less valuable to posterity. The other mood, which pictures all such abuses as things of the past, tends not to reform but only too much to repose; and to the perpetuation of a rather snobbish and paltry version of the Dickensian tradition. In that spirit we may hear to this day a Stiltstalking telling the House of Commons that Stiltstalkings have perished before the march of progress; or in the law courts a Buzfuz quoting Buzfuz and jeering at himself as an extinct monster.

The future of the fame of Dickens is no part of the Dickens record and a very dubious part of the Dickens criticism. Some have suggested that his glory will fade as new fashions succeed those he satirized; others have said, at least equally reasonably, that the difference itself fades when all the fashions have grown old; and that Aristophanes and Cervantes have outlived their descendants as well as their contemporaries. But there can be no question of the importance of Dickens as a human event in history; a sort of conflagration and transfiguration in the very heart of what is called the conventional Victorian era; a naked flame of mere natural genius, breaking out in a man without culture, without tradition, without help from historic religions or philosophies or from the great foreign schools; and revealing a light that never was on sea or land, if only in the long fantastic shadows that it threw from common things.